MY DEAR HEMLOCK

My Dear Hemlock

Tilly Dillehay

CANON PRESS

MOSCOW, IDAHO

Tilly Dillehay, *My Dear Hemlock*

Published by Canon Press
P. O. Box 8729, Moscow, Idaho 83843
800-488-2034 | www.canonpress.com

Cover illustration by Josiah Nance
Cover design by James Engerbretson
Interior design by Valerie Anne Bost
Printed in Canada

ISBN-10: 1-59128-135-0
ISBN-13: 978-1-59128-135-1

Library of Congress Cataloging-in-Publication data is on file with the publisher.

25 26 27 28 29 30 31 32 33   10 9 8 7 6 5 4 3

Contents

For my little women—
Norah, Agnes, and Cordelia

For Spirits, when they please,
Can either sex assume, or both; so soft
And uncompounded is their essence pure . . .

—John Milton, *Paradise Lost*

Foreword

Back in 2019 I received an email from an acquaintance, Tilly Dillehay, to ask if I might be interested in starting a podcast with her. She had a great concept and name already picked out for it: *Home Fires*. It should have been an instant no, since I knew nothing about podcasting and very little about her! Yet, after exchanging many emails and phone calls, I saw what you will likely soon discover if you haven't encountered Tilly before: she is a gem of a sister in Christ, full of insight and honesty.

I was twelve years old when I first read C.S. Lewis's *The Screwtape Letters* at my father's recommendation. It was the first Lewis I had ever read, and from the opening pages I was entranced. He told me things I didn't know about myself. How could he understand the dark inner workings of the heart so well? I believe it's because he was a painfully honest man—honest before God, honest about himself, and an honest observer of others.

Tilly has this rare quality in common with Lewis. She is honest before God and man about herself, she is a keen observer of others, and she translates this honesty into compelling, edifying writing. This means she can tell you things about your own heart and its inner workings that you likely didn't know, things you may not be eager to find out: ugly things, reasons why you're miserable, reasons why you sometimes make others miserable.

But she can also show you how to resist temptation and walk in newness of life as a young woman, a married woman, a mother, and a dying saint. *My Dear Hemlock* is no mere dumpster dive into depravity. As you observe the Patient, you will see a Christian woman's victory—a victory that can be yours in Christ Jesus. Despite the evil designs of the Enemy, the ancient paths of faithfulness have been laid for you to walk on in the obedience of faith.

I think it wise to share the warning Lewis himself wrote in the preface to *Screwtape*:

> There are two equal and opposite errors into which our race can fall about the devils. One is to disbelieve in their existence. The other is to believe, and to feel

> an excessive and unhealthy interest in them. They themselves are equally pleased by both errors and hail a materialist or a magician with the same delight.

Consider yourself duly warned. I imagine there are quite a few more than *two* errors that could be made regarding our thoughts or lack thereof regarding demons. But this isn't really a book about demons at all. It's about you and me.

Having heard Lewis's warnings, I offer two of my own. First, avoid the fault of preferring ignorance about oneself, the fault of the heart that can't bear to be truly examined. Tread no further if your sin is precious to you. Second, once you've pulled the curtains back and let the light come down the cellar steps and watched the cockroaches scurry, don't spend your days going over how many spindly legs they had and how your sin must be uniquely awful in the annals of human history. Just be thankful it's been exposed, repent, and move on. Right seeing is for right living, not for morbid microscopic wallowing in sin. You read these pages with the ready forgiveness of the Father at your side.

That is what this little book of letters between two demons is actually about: *seeing*—seeing the heart of a Christian woman, warts and wonder and everything in between, and, ultimately, seeing the Father's heart for His own.

With deep gratitude,
Abigail Dodds

1

Salutations

My dear Hemlock,

I always enjoy taking on a new mentee—I try to say no, but headquarters just keeps begging. And after all, how can I resist? It's too delightful, putting a new tempter through the paces. How funny they always are! Welcome, darling!

Presumably, you chose the Ministry for the Absorption of Women (MAW) for the same reason I did. You saw early on that the taste of the feminine soul brought some incomparable satisfaction—in short, that it agreed with you. She truly is the glory of man, as even the Enemy has observed, although He could not know the pleasures we have enjoyed in Eve's daughters.

Some tempters overlook this department because they've set their eyes on the heady, but limited, violence of the male sex. They are dazzled by the glories of wars and rapes, eternally attracted to the brute strength of the boardroom and the weight room. But I believe many avoid woman for another reason: they are threatened. Woman, as the Enemy intends her, is a fearsome, nasty, morbid thing, all practicalities and gentleness, the so-called "law of kindness" on her tongue, an interior intractability masked by a kind of calm, maddening hopefulness, courage in the face of despair, lockstep obedience to the Enemy's demands, etc. etc. You've heard the rap sheet before, I dare say.

This only shows you the cowardice of other tempters: they can't handle our specialty. Those who dare little reap little. What they don't understand is the potential for flavor. The taste of a female human is utterly distinct and worth a lifetime of pursuit.

A woman, bent to the will of our Father below, is worthy of any main course: fearful, treacherous, plotting, scheming, lazy, self-indulgent, grasping, terrified of age, duplicitous, despairing, even murderous—the potential for delight is almost endless. What gratification! To bring something so theoretically "lovely" to such treacherous depths.

But I'm getting carried away. I meant to just sit down, say hello, and congratulate you on your choice of discipline.

Sincerely,
Madame Hoaxrot

2

On the Patient's History

My dear Hemlock,

Enclosed is the dossier on your first patient. Her previous caseworker has, as you may have heard, been sent for rehabilitation. Agent Retchworth—lugubrious little worm! From the first you could see he was woefully inept. I have every faith you will do better.

Some damage has already been done. Your patient calls herself a Christian now; our superiors see this as a direct result of Retchworth's incompetence. Early in her life, she appeared to be fairly well in hand, raised by parents who claimed to be in the Enemy's camp but were so hassled by our people as to be innocuous. They did make attempts to shape her conscience along Enemy lines, and they brought her to church often. But the loyalty markers in her home were all of the right kind: pleasure and worldly ambition were the true household gods.

Retchworth made some attempt to take advantage of these inconsistencies. In her teens he called her attention to every possible hypocrisy in the church and in her family but carefully guarded her from glimpsing her own. He invited her to focus on the ineffective faith of her youth and suggested it was really the only kind. She had a nice wobble. She even went so far as to call herself an "agnostic." But this was where Retchworth began to make fatal mistakes.

First he pushed her to develop an intimacy, and then a real affair, with a young man who was a perfect heathen. The idea was to corrupt the girl—and she was indeed corrupted. This young man invested a good deal of time, and her own fleshly appetites helped to draw them together. Because of her churched background, Retchworth found it easy to bring her very far into the debauchery while still convincing her that she was in some sense a believer.

But he overplayed his hand. Retchworth thought she would attach herself to the young man and push off from the mooring of her Christian circles completely. He told me she was ready—after years of groundwork in besetting sin and shame, she would now make the leap and admit she had been on Our Father's side all along. This boyfriend was the perfect helper, Retchworth believed. One of those types who uses long words (she goes in hard for that sort of thing). He made installation art, the best kind—meaningless, tactless, tasteless hunks of metal with lovely "descriptions" describing nothing. His style of talking and writing was gorgeous, built for the obscuration of meaning, but with the tantalizing effect of promise. She would listen to him and feel that, although she hadn't quite gotten to the bottom of his opinions, a bit more time would reveal them. And at any rate, he wore such an open and bright expression on his face when he was talking!

Retchworth spent months writing gleeful reports. But he vastly overestimated the human longing for safety. After a lifetime of having at least one foot in the circle of light, the Patient walked out into the anarchy of the installation artist's worldview and lived for just a few months in a new kind of community. Single, cohabiting, married, with children or without—to a man, the individuals she met seemed to live with their heads bent down into the wind. They all belonged to us. She saw that supreme pragmatism in their eyes, that prudent impermanence in their relationships. Their grasp of right and wrong was as slippery as hers. She ought to have embraced this freedom.

She did not.

My belief is that she simply couldn't take it. She wasn't strong enough. She couldn't accept the lightless world, not at this stage in her development. She positively *cringed* back to the Enemy, scuttled back into the circle of light like a cockroach in reverse. Retchworth now knows firsthand something he totally overlooked: fear, though a great ally in our Father's warfare, can sometimes yield quite negative consequences.

Another momentous mistake from R: he threw up his hands, confident and jovial, and said, "Let her go," when her parents proposed that she live for a few weeks with a pastor's family and "counsel" with them. R seemed to think this no object. He wrote to me at the time: "She is only going to see more of the Christian rigmarole . . . they want to separate her from her lover, which I think will be a useful opposition in a moment when she might be in danger of seeing the relationship in more of a sordid than a romantic light . . . anyway, a little hope now and then never hurts them; only lays down sediment for the stone layers of future despair . . ."

He was a fool. In retrospect, I believe this was a failure of research, mainly. If he had looked into the kind of place she was going, he would have called in reinforcements immediately to work on the parents, on the boyfriend, on anybody at all to prevent her going. Surely, even he would have had the imagination to see what kind of contrast she was set up to notice. And it *was* a setup on the part of the Enemy; in his self-justifying report, Retchworth at least hit on that much. We now believe the Enemy deliberately called her bluff by letting her spend so much time among those further down the road to Chaos. Then He set her down in . . . a home, of all places.

A home of the worst kind. Here she saw peace, and laughter, and the fruit of long years of ministry and commitment.

She was hugged by a woman with another kind of open and bright expression. She was listened to. The Enemy's book was opened to her.

One of R's big protests later on was, "She already saw the book! She saw it a thousand times and heard it! How could I (or anyone) know it would be dangerous to her now? One can never tell when the Enemy will run a stealth operation of this kind . . ." His implication (self-justifying, of course) was that the Enemy always gets His man—that the Enemy lulls us into false security by letting patients hear the book read a million times without being changed, and then snaps His fingers and lights them up from within, like Edison's bulb.

Treasonous conspiracy theories of this kind get traction from time to time, usually revived by pathetic, trembling demons like R in the throes of failure. You would never stoop to such excuse-making, I am sure. Take your punishment; take it like a woman, I always say.

But this department has by no means despaired of her soul. Indeed, we have only just begun. We suspect the so-called "conversion" is in this case of the most pragmatic sort. Motivated by fear of the great floor-less, wall-less, ceiling-less Void, she crept back under the Oppressive Wing. But give her a few months in captivity, and we believe she will begin to yearn for the freedom of Chaos again.

Sincerely,
Madame Hoaxrot

P.S. I haven't been acquainted with your own history as yet. Perhaps you could tell me a bit about yourself and your previous assignments? How is it that you come to be in need of instruction this late in the game? I am always happy to educate; but some background knowledge helps. Commander Millstone was remarkably demure on the subject.

3

On Newlyweds

My dear Hemlock,

So she married one of them.

I can tell you're feeling a bit nauseous, fresh from having attended the wedding and heard a lecture about the Enemy's disgusting plans to "marry" His own bride. It's disconcerting, I know, when you must listen to the vows the clumps of tissue make to one another, and you start to have dizzying thoughts of what would happen if they actually *kept* them.

Fortunately, they seldom do.

There's much fun to be had here, Hemlock. Marriage in itself is not something we approve of. But your report on the two honeymooners is most encouraging, most auspicious. Two months in, nestled like lovebirds into their little apartment, and they are already in that state of shock that is so entertaining to observe in the newlywed.

She's becoming vaguely dismayed that her young husband seems to have forgotten his indebtedness to her for marrying him. He's beginning to suspect that her adoring gaze did not come with a lifetime guarantee. Is she not, he wonders, entirely the sweet and cheerful girl he had been led to believe? Is he not, she wonders, quite the man of action and decision she was drawn to—but a slobby man, a man who watches TV more nights than he should, who leaves his underwear in strange places and clearly has no intention of ever learning to load the dishwasher?

No one is watching them now, you see. They are not the bride and groom, surrounded by photographers and cakes, envious friends and gratified family. Now they are only Him and Her, Adam and Eve. And although they're still amazed at being allowed to just hang around alone together, with or without clothing, boredom and annoyance already begin to rob them of their newfound delight.

Some of these carts push themselves, but don't be complacent at this juncture. In itself, the disappointment is no victory at all; it is a foregone conclusion any time two creatures say vows and shack up. But *the way they respond to* this disappointment is like the setting of a bone after a fracture. Their habits will harden into a certain position in the honeymoon season, and the result will be either long-term soundness and strength, aiding Enemy operations enormously, or a gorgeous, lifelong limp that you will use to weaken them in every other area of life.

Here are some of my favorite ways to set these fractures at a nice jaunty angle. (Of course, you'll need to be working closely with Malindulge, who oversees the husband. But he will have been in touch.)

1. *Solidify the Patient's belief that, in order to praise* anything *about her husband, she must be in total approval of* everything *about him.*

Humans are always uncomfortably aware of their own dissatisfaction with another person—and they like to wait for that discomfort to clear so that they can be "perfectly honest" when they offer positive feedback. Every time they witness something praiseworthy, their eyes are drawn immediately to a dozen other things with which to find fault. They conclude that praising the one praiseworthy thing would in some sense excuse or incentivize the other reprehensible things. (Interestingly, they are not so concerned about criticizing too freely while "dishonestly" overlooking praiseworthy items.)

For her, to say, "Thank you for taking out the trash," would be to imply that she didn't notice how he left his plate on the counter and the toilet seat up. And to say, "Thank you for working so hard at your job; you're good at what you do; I'm so lucky to have you," would feel tantamount to whitewashing every sin, every folly, and every idiosyncrasy she's noticed since they got married.

It's quite simple to encourage her in this belief, to make the praise stick in her throat. Incite her to build up an imaginary man in her mind—a flawless captain she knows she *could* passionately, unreservedly, and wholeheartedly commend in every area of life. Then encourage her to wait for this man to arrive on the scene before she opens her mouth in praise.

You want to get her into the headspace that says, *Until he earns it, I will not give it.* This applies to more than just praise—she can be taught to do the same with sex, obedience, good food, really anything at all that the Enemy asks her to cheerfully offer. This is by far the most desirable response from a woman when the inevitable marital disappointments come: a kind of tight-lipped, crossed-armed, toe-tapping posture toward her spouse. She can wait a long, long time.

We must do everything in our power to prevent her finding out a standard fact about the male human: he will usually slouch to meet a woman's disapproval and grow to meet her praise. Men simply don't respond to criticism the way women believe they will. It's the old Aesop's fable about the sun and the wind in a contest to remove a man's coat. Our best marriages occur when a woman is constantly trying the wind's method, blowing as cold and hard as she can. Husbands universally respond by pulling their coats tighter around them. (In the fable, the sun shines warmly on the man's face so that he removes the coat voluntarily. It is a dangerous secret, really.)

One word of praise would do much more to "improve" him than a hundred critical words ever could. But it would also change *her*. Giving thanks produces a habit of thankfulness. Gratitude begets more pernicious gratitude.

This dangerous principle is the same principle that—writ large—could really lose a crucial piece of ground for you. So take care that you start with disapproval of the husband and expand it. You want her to look at the Enemy and say exactly the same thing that she says to hubby: *Until You please me, I will not praise you. Until You make my life easier, I will not give thanks. Until You give me joy, I will not be so dishonest as to sing a psalm.*

In this way, you will produce a gorgeous flush of silent disapproval that takes in her entire world. All of the Enemy's works will evaporate in the stunning silence of an ungrateful disposition, a thanks unspoken. Whether it be a sunny day, a hot shower, a pancake, a new baby, or a husband, the Enemy's "gifts" will be met with the pursed lips of one who is waiting to see an unbroken vista of perfection—a life that meets entirely with her approval—before she plucks up the one blessing and names it in gratitude.

2. *Teach her to overlook the common courtesies.*

Politeness—one of those things in marriage that can create an insufferably pleasant time for decades and decades of life together—she will want to totally overlook. A please, a thank you, a kiss goodbye, a greeting hello, a napkin handed over at the table: the sorts of things she would take care to offer another human in their home, you want her to withhold from her own spouse.

Basic courtesy, which would grease the skids of both their everyday life together and their more serious trials, you can teach her to discount as below her notice. You can then replace it with real inattention, which will detract from the good times and make the hard times harder.

Eventually any human comes to resent living with another human who doesn't seem to notice or care for them in even the most elementary ways. Resentment will escalate simple inattention to positive rudeness.

Then, when she becomes dissatisfied with the resulting temperature of their home, teach her to cast about for more complicated, more clinical answers. This will be quite easy. When there is trouble, humans always prefer a huge overhaul or a complicated theory to a simple task. Someone may suggest something too obvious, something like, "Kiss each other goodbye every day when one of you leaves and say hello when one of you returns." And she will snort that the person making the suggestion simply doesn't understand the problem. The humans are all Naamans, certain that their problems are too unique and too knotty for a simple swim in the Jordan.

3. *Encourage her to make a habit of setting spiritual goals for her husband rather than for herself.*

She is such a baby Christian that she has no idea how baby a Christian she is. She certainly can't see that her husband is actually further along. Here it is very entertaining to take advantage of the human tendency to learn a new obedience one moment and then, in the exact next moment, look angrily around at people who don't seem as obedient about the same thing.

She learned to pray about five minutes ago, and for the first time in her life, she is in an active season of disciplined morning prayer. But even though she is wobbling around on new legs, doing something totally unfamiliar, she's already looking at her husband in the mornings with the suspicion that he doesn't have good prayer habits!

This sort of girl will always attempt to teach something before she has finished learning it, will always try to hold others to a standard that she herself is going to go slack on in about a month, and will be perfectly unaware of her own hypocrisy. Encourage this sidelong glance, and you'll produce a kind of spiritual six-year-old in the back seat, telling tales on her brother during the long car ride home.

Discourage her from actually praying *for* her husband. This is really just unhelpful all around. Instead, encourage her to fret, mumble under her breath, and worry for him. She should carry around resentments over his shortcomings, wring her hands helplessly over his social gaffes and the habits he picked up from his father, give him evenings of silence over faults that he has no idea he has. But she must never pray about these things.

That's all for now. And listen, don't worry about the sex; I know it's a little troubling at first. Hard to wrap your mind around what's happening, when it seems to open them up to some new brand of bliss and a kind of untouchable distraction in each other. We suspect HIS motives in it all—why the intolerably permissive attitude toward something that takes them so far beyond the pale of the "suffering servant" shtick? It seems obvious that the creatures lose their heads completely in these moments. Disgusting, copulating little beasts, and He hasn't a word to say to them except "Go to, and be blessed."

But this sort of thing often blows over in a marriage. Give it six months, and then you can start to produce a crop of sexlessness with greater success. More on this later.

Sincerely,
Madame Hoaxrot

4

On Confession of Sin

My dear Hemlock,

I'll answer your first question first. You asked which is better: to encourage your woman to start a fight with the husband about what he did, or to encourage her to ignore what he did and punish him with silence. The answer is—yes.

Honestly, it's little matter to me which she does, as long as her heart is cooled and hardened toward her husband and the Enemy. So choose the one that comes most naturally to her, and let her flesh do the work. If she's a natural fighter, send her into the ring with gloves on, tongue unloosed; if she's a stuffer, make sure she has plenty to stew on and then leave her alone to line up his faults and count them.

Either option is golden. Choose your pleasure. But the thing you must really take care to avoid is confession of sin.

You've probably heard that we don't know precisely how confession works. In most cases, everyone involved already knows about the sin. The Enemy certainly does—He doesn't need the human creatures to tell Him. They themselves know (at least vaguely)—how else could they confess it? And the other people closest to them, the ones harmed by the sin—they usually know as well.

So the procedure is not, apparently, about the passing of information. It's not a memo. It's another kind of transaction entirely. Some kind of hateful ritual the Enemy has dreamed up.

Research is still working on the exact method He uses to unlock the cages around human hearts. But that is what confession does, that much we know. It is a horrible, spiteful trick on His part, a key by which the rodents break out of the most well-defended personal cages we construct! I have had patients escape a five-year steel trap of depression and despair, many feet thick, by the simple discovery that they could confess specific sin, right when it happened, to the Enemy and to the people they sinned against.

It's deceptively simple, and wildly frustrating.

Confession is to be avoided whenever possible. So let me outline the two major categories of sin and what tactics to use with each of them:

1. *Big secret sins.* These are the sins of shadow, the sins of life-domination, the ones with great big hooks in the flesh. The ones she is deeply ashamed of, that perhaps exist from her anxious teenage years or from her debuached young adulthood. Rage episodes, drunkenness, pornography, drugs—that sort of lineup. You know as well as I do that this is where our most legendary stars built their empires: Prednometh, Fructigoth, Shiva, all those junior tempters who got the Google search engine assignment . . . fortunes have been made. Young tempters get all starry-eyed over the glamour of this category, but many of us make a very good living in the bread and butters:

2. *Everyday sins against her fellow man.* This is the gossip over the water cooler, the rude comment to her husband, the angry word to her child, the disrespectful remark to her mother. She will be doing these things every day to some degree, and so they are easy for her to overlook. Much potential!

It is not so very complicated to get her to keep these things entirely to herself. Take the #1 category:

For starters, she will be very unwilling to confess this kind of sin to another person. Her husband or her mentor will rise obviously to her mind as the person she MIGHT confess to. *But is it necessary?* you will whisper. She can sit in the question of necessity for a long time. Get her to wait as long as possible, hoping time will take care of the problem by lessening the guilt. (It will, but not in the way she would perhaps desire; she'll get gradual relief, but it will be because her nerve endings, her guilt mechanism—in fact, her conscience—has begun to wear out.)

This anxious waffling on the question of confessing to another human is also a way we have of pulling her eyes off of the Enemy's clear view of her. If she does begin to consider confession to her husband or her mentor, she'll often think of it in terms of penance: "Confession is hard, indeed it is most unpleasant, but it is the price God wants me to pay for my sin." We want her to forget what we cannot—the Enemy sees her at all times. He not only knows every detail of her behavior, but He claims to have set up a legal loophole to absolve her of it. He claims to have already "paid the price" for her drunken stupor, her night of lustful escape.

So you'll want to interrupt this process at every possible point. If she must confess, let her do the first (to the Enemy) without doing the second (to another person), or the second (to another person) without doing the first (to the Enemy). Delay her in either or both of these steps as long as possible, and often she will have a "bad season" caused by her conscience in distress, followed by a season when she pulls herself back into the road of grace, doing her best to forget her "fall" and do better. Get her to delay again and again, and you've really got her; but even getting her to delay and confess only after a few episodes is good. She loses time that way, you see. Lots of time.

There is also a very entertaining mathematical operation you'll find her ready to perform with you: reducing the severity of a major sin episode by about 30 percent in the confession. It's remarkable how common this is, and it is of great use to us. Remember that they will have a sore, inflamed conscience, and so they will be looking for ways to soothe it. So sometimes it is actually safer to indulge her in the relief of a "confession" that is actually another sin: a new lie about the extent of the sin, told at the very moment of trying to unburden herself! Just a little touch of brake, right at the end, when she is in danger of being shed of the whole episode—take advantage of this whenever you can.

I've suddenly been overcome by ennui. I will finish next week, or when it suits me.

Sincerely,
Madame Hoaxrot

5

On Confession of Sin, Cont'd

My dear Hemlock,

I believe I was elucidating the two categories of human sin, with confession-prevention strategies for each. Having covered #1 (Big Secret Sins) with typically elegant prose and crisp insight, I now turn to #2 (Everyday Sins).

In the case of the everyday sins your patient commits against her husband or her coworkers, our tactic is still to delay confession (what else?)—but the delay feels very different for her. She knows they know what she did. They're the ones she did it to. That tone of voice, used to let her husband know what she thinks of him—if it didn't communicate clearly, she wouldn't use it! That pettish, punishing silence she used on her sister for an entire afternoon—obviously she meant it to sting. But if she's gotten over it and they've both "moved on," why say anything about it?

This is the kind of delay we generally rely on for #2 sins: "But it was only . . ." If #1 sins go unconfessed because they feel too great, #2 sins go unconfessed because they feel too small. You can get her to think, "I do this every day. You can't go through a big conversation every time, can you?"

You see? This way, you get her to pile up months of crusted-over "small" sins. She and her husband will go picking their way around the piles, stepping on old trash left from a silent supper three months ago, and they'll stop noticing it's even there. As long as they never begin the habit of confession, they'll build this delightful tartar of the soul for years.

This is how hatred begins, Hemlock. Don't underestimate it.

Because one clear confession does more than enough heavy lifting for the sixty or so seconds it requires. For one thing, it acknowledges that the behavior in question has been officially flagged "sin." Nobody can hide behind "But it was only . . ." And it means that, next time, both of them are aware that the behavior in question was recently named "sin" and can be regarded as such. Calling sin "sin" is deplorably freeing to both the sinner and the sinned against.

You remember learning that the humans were given an imprint of that stiff tyranny the Enemy calls Truth. They were made to respond to the stuff. On the plus side, this means we can steal their joy by bits and shreds even if they simply shade or obscure the thing He calls Truth. We love to take advantage of this. It's so effective—the smallest lie about something absolutely immaterial causes real damage because of the Enemy's imprint.

But unfortunately, this same principle works in reverse. Allow them to name and clarify something the Enemy would call "true," and the vermin's eyes actually *see better*. When they confess wrongdoing, another layer of murky glass falls from their faces, and the effect spreads to all of life, not just the area affected by the confession. They actually become *smarter*. So does the human to whom they are confessing.

Distract, delay, discourage—do whatever you have to do, but don't allow your girl to set up a habit of confessing small sins. Keep the memory of her wrongdoing just at the periphery. Give her just enough awareness to try to "do better," to climb out of the situation by forcing herself into a calmer mood, changing the scene, or getting on her phone for distraction. Put a little distance between her and the moment, and you can guide her smoothly into the next temptation, burdened and unarmed.

This kind of nerve damage can reach truly advanced stages without killing the creature. You've heard of these sorts of cases before, I imagine: a high-profile minister suddenly revealed as an embezzler, a happy church deacon arrested for child porn, a homeschooling mom sent to rehab for opioids. The world hails the moment of explosion as the great moment of our victory—the point where these people "fell into sin" and were subsequently unmasked. But you and I know that by the time they're found out, the best part of the feast is over.

The purest delicacy on the fat soul of a religious person is that crusty layer of conscience, seared. A conscience like that takes years of watching and nudging as it cooks itself to the perfect shade of black. What flavor! And the despair we nibble on, for year after year after year, as the victim sinks further and further into his secrets, obsessions, dominating habits! There's no hypocrite like a religious hypocrite, I always say.

Your girl has all the same potential for flavor. If you can get her to overlook sin, to hide sin, to laugh at sin, and to isolate herself in the struggle against sin, you have already lowered her onto the coals. Her spiritual nerve endings will be damaged every time she deliberately silences them. She will suffer—how she will suffer!

But if she ever gets to realize she could live day in and day out with a clear conscience—woe betide you. The shame we enjoy in most human beings would dry up. And then what? Intimacy, almost uninterrupted intimacy with the Enemy. A screen, blocking your access, a barrier against which you may tear your fingernails for the next fifty years.

Sincerely,
Madame Hoaxrot

6

On Prayer

My dear Hemlock,

I was on vacation last week, inhabiting the front left wheel of a Walmart shopping cart. Thoroughly enjoyed.

Your questions about what to "do with yourself" while the Patient is praying show me where you are. You know less than I thought and lack the instincts I had hoped for.

What to do with yourself? What to do with *yourself*? Did you pull up a pillow for her—dim the lights, bring her a cool drink of water?

Poor, sad thing. I suppose it never entered your despicable little head to *do your job*. Do you imagine prayer time is your quick break in between real activity? And you stand in a corner, abashed, utterly overcome, wondering "what to do with yourself"! The obvious presence of the Enemy should have put you immediately on the offensive. Three things I'd like you to keep in mind from here on out:

1. *Distraction is always your first move.*

Begin immediately implementing the standard tactic of intrusive thoughts, alternating between the mundane, the accusatory, and the worldly.

Don't imagine that you're sitting at the girl's ear, whispering, "Don't pray, don't pray, don't pray, don't pray." Distraction is always the way. Intrude on her train of thought. Tap her, incessantly tap her. Whether it's the laundry, the phone, even the Book itself, suggest gently that there is something else she should be doing. Then help her to vaguely feel that, if she did try to pray, she would not be quite in her best form, that she is not quite feeling fresh and innocent and pious enough to approach the throne of the "One True [censored]."

It is generality we thrive on here, Hemlock. We don't care how often she resolves to "pray more"; we don't care how many friends she promises, "I'll pray for you." Just see that she doesn't allow structure into her prayer life, structure that will put her through the early years of not yet really liking to pray, and not yet feeling like she's "good" at it. Never let her ask the obvious question of how and when she will pray. In short, just see she doesn't actually do any praying.

Your girl's inexperience is obvious. When she tries to pray, she stumbles through a list of requests and can't even quite tell what to ask for in each case: "Lord, please heal so-and-so; Father, please save so-and-so." She confesses a bit. She reaches for something to say about the Enemy Himself: "Father, you are so, so good . . ." And throughout the prayer, she feels she ought to say *more*, because her thoughts seem very short and inadequate, and the pastor at church seems to say a lot more than she does. But while she is thinking of what to say next, she loses her train of thought and half-heartedly opens the Book again. She is easily fuddled and very easily distracted, and you will find it quite simple to help her go weeks at a time without making much contact.

Her grandmother, a Christian as well, lived among people who understood that prayer was not a romantic activity but an essential and ordinary routine, like milking the cow every day. It was a matter of course that prayer would take work and repetition and that it would be done by normal Christians everywhere. People at that time used phrases like "say your prayers," which to today's human ears sounds dreadfully wooden.

Your patient's generation of Christians seems to be holding out for something better than just "saying their prayers." They intend their prayers to be very heartfelt, very well said, and very long. And while they are waiting for such prayers to overtake them, they can often be induced not to pray at all.

Keep up that natural abhorrence to the rote, the childlike, the brief. Keep her from focusing her efforts on any of the nursery rhymes He gave them (the Enemy's Prayer, all those ghastly psalms, etc.).

2. *Protect her from anyone who shows a dangerous tendency to direct or instruct.*

This should not be difficult. Odds are, even in her church, no other Christian has looked her in the eye and said, "You should learn to pray." Fewer and fewer Christian women feel the liberty to say things like that to each other. Speaking with authority of any kind is rather frowned upon these days. It isn't fashionable to keep up appearances as her grandmother would have done. Your patient lives among women who are all hunched, who carefully guard against the appearance of showing off by wearing spiritual flats.

In fact we have brought them to a point where any kind of advice must be given in a very self-abusing way, if it is given at all. We have them apologetically admitting to an organized laundry system or meal plan, a clean closet or a sleep-trained infant. Obviously, this is a useful way to weaken human effort in any practical area of life. But we have had our greatest success using it to weaken the spiritual disciplines.

"The Christian life involves reading the Bible and praying each day." Such a simple statement cannot be made without implying that the *speaker* is reading the Bible and praying. And what is that but pharisaism? Aghast, some Christians will guard themselves carefully from such concrete language. However, if a woman publicly declares she hasn't mopped her floor in a year and can't ever find time to pick up a Bible, she'll be met with laughter and rejoicing.

And so, in this tidy little stalemate, your new Christian patient won't often come across an older woman who's offering to teach her to pray—if indeed the older Christians around her even know how.

3. *Identify the Patient's ditch and push her into it.*

You seem very concerned about the habit she's picked up of reading Enemy material. And, of course, you are right to feel dread and alarm over this pernicious problem. Reading the Enemy's book is not something you can necessarily keep her from doing if all of her friends are doing it. It's one of those cultural diseases that a patient sometimes picks up, like the measles. But I wouldn't throw up your hands too soon. The many alarming things she will pick up in her reading can be dimmed quite a bit if you interfere effectively with prayer.

Most churches have one of two emphases: either they emphasize the Book (the reading and understanding of it), or they emphasize encounters with the "Holy Spirit" (part of the Enemy's ever-slippery personality), primarily through prayer. Studious vs. Spiritual, you might say.

You may think it matters little which emphasis your girl and her church tend to, because they're both hateful. But the fact is, we must understand the direction she leans, because that's the direction we want to push. You are going for a level of emphasis that amounts to an imbalance. In the case of your girl, she is probably going to continue her habit of Bible reading for the present. You are decidedly dealing with a group on the Studious end of the spectrum.

But she is likely to be weak in her knowledge of the Enemy Spirit. She won't expect present-day interventions on the part of the Enemy. Her people tend to believe—subconsciously, of course—that most of His biggest work was finished up about two thousand years ago. Discourage prayer, and you will reinforce these unexamined assumptions. Every episode of reading the book can thus be undercut. Yes, make prayer your hill to die on.

Prayer would be an unfortunate key to her. It would combine the insidious power of the Book with a relationship built; she would begin to see and hear things. If the book is the Enemy's propaganda poster, the opening of state secrets to the average piddling little soldier, prayer is the Commander-in-Chief's personal telephone number, a handwritten invitation to sit in His chamber for a meal and a chat. The Book makes believers; prayer seems to make radicals. It produces people who don't just claim but actually appear to *believe* that they are in a war. (They also become increasingly delusional about one side or the other "winning," but that is a topic for another day.)

Book reading can be dangerous. But prayer is the beginning of the end of your work with this girl.

I see one worrisome detail here—there is a prayer meeting at her church. Indeed, it almost looks like a group that wants to combine the two emphases. I'm sure you can imagine why these simple meetings with older believers are the sort we abhor. You have doubtless experienced the effects—the weakness, the inertia. Not to mention the smell.

But if you imagine she will automatically take these habits home to her bedroom, you are wholly mistaken. This is exactly where the rubber meets the road, and where your job is only just beginning. Even you will not find it terribly difficult.

Without another human witness, she won't know when the prayer stops and the daydreaming begins. If you can keep that clarity from reaching her, you'll have nothing to fear from her little "prayer" times. They will soon cease. She won't be able to sustain something that has no beginning or end, and no clear aim. No one can. Her prayer life will then subside into the kind we like best (if it *must* happen): prayerful feelings, attempted on the run or in passing, mustered by emotion, need, or guilt, and never expected to do much.

One last thing: encourage nonspecific requests whenever possible. With these, the humans never have to wrestle with why the Enemy said no, and they'll always wonder if He's ever said yes. They'll never trust a beam that hasn't held their weight before. And as long as they never test its weight by standing on it, the beam will always remain untrustworthy.

If she remains with the Enemy for very long, she's bound to pick prayer up eventually. You can't prevent it forever. But delay, delay—delay the inevitable, my dear Hemlock, as long as you can. Most of our work consists in delaying the inevitable.

I spy that pathetic little worm, Murkwood; time for some fun. The weak, blubbering little thing!

Sincerely,
Madame Hoaxrot

P.S. Try to prevent her praying on her knees or whispering aloud. Harder to "peter out" the prayer . . .

P.P.S. We enjoy having the humans *promise* to pray for each other. It makes liars out of most of them. Your girl will have already learned to say "I'll pray for you" at the end of a Christianesey conversation. As a meaningless but very sincere closer, it almost ensures forgetfulness and later, vague guilt for a broken promise. But take care she never acquires the dreadful habit one of my patients picked up: she started praying with the person right *then and there*! It was ghastly, and once set into motion, unstoppable. We looked on in consternation as her friends started doing the same.

P.P.P.S. At the end of this letter, I see I made a statement that may expose me to unpleasant assumptions on your part. When I said that much of our work is in delay—and that often this is the delay of the inevitable—it may have sounded like I was talking about our Great Cause. But I was talking about the particulars of temptation, not of the War itself! And if you try to report any of this to the Intelligence Below, I think you can see you'll be disappointed; my statements are always vetted for accuracy. (Not that you would! xoxoxoxo)

7

On "Marrying Down"

My dear Hemlock,

I thought of something for your girl. It's an easy tactic for any tempter, and she seems like the ideal candidate.

When you have a pretty woman marrying a nice, average, hardworking young man, I've had much success inviting her to think often of how the young man "married up."

You might think your patient would shrink from such an idea, finding it vulgar and economical. After all, marriage, according to human dogma, is supposed to be an exchange of free love and commitment, not an exchange on the stock market. But the thing is, most humans think of marriage exactly as we think of it: an exchange of goods and services for other goods and services. They don't know that they think this, because many of them are in the heightened emotional state they call "being in love" when they choose to get married. But for most of history, they believed it, and they knew they believed it: marriage was a kind of "buying in." You hoped to buy in at the highest possible level—someone with as many pigs as possible, as large a hut as possible, as important a family name as possible, etc.

In the place and time your girl occupies, the humans don't admit to themselves or others that they believe they are "buying in." But they still believe it. They want someone who comes with the highest concentration of commodities possible: the commodities being physical attractiveness, social clout, money, exciting conversation, interesting hobbies, and so on. Without these commodities, none of them could be induced to marry. Even when they say they "love" another person, what they generally mean is that they love the qualities in the person that make them feel important by association, or that they love the life the person will probably give them.

With this kind of setup, there are all kinds of delightful results. One of the most obvious is the one I wrote about in one of my first letters, i.e., the surprise and disappointment when they enter real life and discover the disconnect between expectation and reality. He finds out that she actually has a rather critical opinion of his Lego collection. She finds out that the five jokes he won her heart with are his entire repertoire. Buyer's remorse, you know. The broken bone that I spoke of earlier.

What I'm offering now is a particularly entertaining tip in the bone-setting genre, guaranteeing future pain. One of you (yourself or Malindulge) must get your patient to believe deeply that, in the market exchange, they have genuinely "married down." In this case, I think it should be your move; your girl is more foolish than the man, and she'd go for it. Also in your favor is the fact that she's pretty.

Oh, I do enjoy this one. In this recipe, we simmer the discontent of disappointed premarital expectations, then blend it with an irrational expectation of fame.

The human desire to be swept away—to be delivered from mundane difficulties into another life—has always been among them. We have always targeted any remotely pretty woman by suggesting that "with her face, perhaps her boring and difficult life could have been different"—if she'd married the richer man in the village, if the prince had only shown up at her door.

But a hundred years ago, when photography and movies started getting big, this narrative took on another layer of plausibility. Human beings routinely became a sort of "graven image" at the touch of a button! Suddenly, fame was no longer only the province of gods and emperors. Even young girls yearned to participate in it—*and really believed they could.*

It used to be difficult to sustain a woman's belief that the rich man in the village might have married her; there are only so many rich men to go around. But now, a pretty woman can treasure another fictional life in her heart for years with perfect confidence, the life of a "famous" woman. She has seen images of famous women on screen and in print every day of her life, and you can bet that, at least once in her life, someone has told her she could be one of those women. Even if the idea is farfetched, she can be made to always wonder.

Now, of course, we have still another incredible development. Social media has made it possible for her to *do* something, to take concrete steps to pursue the fame she desires. Almost every woman we work with these days is actually creating images of herself that are oh-so-similar to the ones she sees of the actually *famous* women. She's "in the pictures"! (Only she's the one taking the pictures, and she's usually the main person looking at them.)

A select few have used social media to carve out a certain kind of fame for themselves, with real currency changing hands. This makes the illusion of fame, just beyond grasp, so incredibly, satisfyingly sustainable. It's a feast, an absolute smorgasbord, of desperation, false hope, and wasted energy. You'll see.

This endless tease serves all kinds of useful ends: promoting discontentment (primarily with the Enemy Himself), spiritual boredom, defiant pride and snobbish disregard for others, despair over unrealized dreams, etc. etc. But it carries a particular benefit for her marriage.

To the flesh of a woman feeding on the fame dream, the eyes of her husband will never be enough. You want to press on that. In her voracious appetite for *fame*, the eyes of her husband, even if enthusiastically turned in her direction, will feel like small potatoes. She wants more. She lusts to be lusted after. Mixed up in this desire for male regard is the more fundamental desire to be admired by anyone and everyone, for any quality at all. And her husband's eyes will never provide the inflation of regard she requires.

The strange but very useful thing about this is that *she will actually resent him for it.*

After laying her whole sense of importance and value at her husband's feet, after demanding that he be a king in order to set off her queenliness to advantage, she will be mortified and chagrined when he turns out to be just a regular man who wants to live a regular life.

The disappointment can be maintained for much longer than you'd think. She can take the bitterness of this one thing—being forced to live a normal life with a normal man—to the grave. I have seen women in their sixties still living in the shell shock of surprise that they aren't movie stars, that they have to clean their own bathrooms, and that their husbands dare to age and grow fat like other men.

Now, if your patient were to take this insatiable appetite down to the studs, she would find one dangerous nugget of information. The appetite is actually an indicator of something I believe the Enemy intended for His own pernicious purposes. Her appetite to be seen may be an indicator of His intention to *look at her*—He Himself.

Of course, if she were to get carried away and become enamored of this idea, it would show her native human naivete—she should really ask herself whether she actually *wants* His horrifying gaze. For those humans who think they do want such an experience, I sometimes think, let the fools have it. They'll deserve what they have coming when He destroys them with a look (after giving them the desire for the look in the first place). More of the same with Him. From the beginning He has done so: forever planting the desire for the impossible into the hearts of His creatures and then punishing us for wanting things.

Anyway, it's best to muddy any connection in her mind between this insatiable desire and the Enemy's eye. Instead, she must be encouraged to dwell on the husband—why does he continue to fail in making her feel admired enough, *seen* enough? Why did she marry down in the first place? Why didn't she hold out for better?

After years of this delightful circle of thought, I have had patients in my care walk away from decades-long marriages, sure that they'll find something better. And then, out in the wide world, either they make exactly the same mistakes over again with a new husband, or they suddenly, tragically see a long list of wonderful qualities in their husband they never saw before.

The thing is, women are wonderful at pinpointing the missing qualities in their menfolk. It really doesn't matter what kind of man your girl is married to; she will be equipped and ready to discover all the qualities he doesn't have and to imagine how desirable these qualities must be in a husband. If he is a steady, plodding worker, she will think of the excitement of being married to an entrepreneur! If she has a fun, life-of-the-party man, she will think longingly of the serious, brooding, intelligent type! If she has married the easygoing man, she'll wish he would just show his authority now and then—and if he ever shows his authority, Enemy help him!

It's delightful, the endless iterations of this game. And then, if Malindulge gets the man well in hand and he sins against her in some truly spectacular way—infidelity, heavy drinking, fits of rage, etc.—we have several very satisfying directions open to us.

Her new male friend at the office should prove a useful foil. How different he is from her husband! (Let her count the ways!)

Sincerely,
Madame Hoaxrot

8

On the Emotional Affair

My dear Hemlock,

The situation at the office seems to have heated up to an indistinct simmer. I see potential, if not for an immediate blow-up of her whole marriage, then at least for a long-standing episode of unarticulated lust. This exercise, because it would be conducted almost entirely in the confines of her own mind, would keep her safely distant from the Enemy for a protracted period without scaring her enough to wake her up to her danger.

Both in the case of transgression and in the case of virtue, she is never sure whether the mind or the body "counts" more. So you may find her overeating or overdrinking, for instance, and even if her conscience bothers her about it, she will be quite ready to accept your whispered reassurances that what she does with her body is not the main thing. After all, her mind, her soul is what matters! Her intention is the important bit; she must only see that her *heart* is pure (even if her appetites are completely out of control!). Here she will call to mind some lines about how "everything created by God is good, and nothing is to be rejected." (She doesn't often finish this quote in her mind, the "with thanksgiving" part.)

On the other hand, when she dallies with the pleasurable sensations caused by wondering whether her coworker did, in fact, *mean* something by that instant-too-long eye contact yesterday, she will then use exactly the opposite argument on herself and never notice the ironic reversal she has achieved. As she slides without much struggle into a profound episode of lustful thoughts, she will tell herself vaguely, "It's not as if I'm having a *real* affair. Of course it would be different if he actually *did* something, or said something, and I didn't stop him. This is just me trying to assess the situation." And she will quite forget the things she told herself before, about the heart being the important bit.

A woman's lust! What an art of subtle misdirection! I won't say it's easier to maintain than the man's lust, necessarily (the male preoccupation never seems to age, and the asinine gloatings in those departments are laughable—only a demon who has never known self-awareness would brag so much over accomplishing modest goals in the EASIEST JOB

ON THE FORCE). But a woman's lust is uniquely sustainable because you can hide it so well from the woman herself.

The reason a woman can overlook her lust is that she's not usually preoccupying herself with parts of the man *per se*. A man in lust imagines bouncing breasts and preoccupies himself with the mechanical manipulations thereof (gag). He then experiences physical reactions that even so simple a creature as himself can't ignore. Subtle? Not hardly. He may not know the word "lust," but he isn't much confused about the territory he finds himself in.

The woman, on the other hand, may not ever notice the ground she stands on, because she rarely thinks longing thoughts about the genitalia of the male in question. In fact, she is vaguely put off by those physical parts of him, unless a great deal of physical interaction is already underway.

Instead, she is mostly preoccupied with *his whole human self, gazing at her whole human self and being utterly taken with it*. She lusts to be lusted after, remember. So when she imagines the tête-à-têtes between herself and her coworker, much of the fantasy is unspoken, expressed in body language, or in barely suppressed confessions, not of mere desire but of deep and advanced "love."

Since she is now married and he is engaged to someone else, she must by necessity detach her ideas of "love" from the duties of married people. She must find a way to separate the idea of "love" from fidelity, financial support, and childrearing; because, at this point, she is unwilling to imagine the two of them abandoning their very new commitments for another in-kind commitment. It would feel rather cheap, you know.

So instead, the "love" confessed must be a Frankenstein's monster of her own making, collaged together out of 1990s romantic comedy films, Jane Austen novels, and Christian ideas of sacrifice. The man in her fantasy turns to her and says something like "I wish we could, but we mustn't. Ah, but I've never met anyone like you!" And so her delicate aversion to adultery is never violated by the man of her imagination. And yet, in her fantasy, he is somehow able to communicate that he does want her, that he cherishes her utterly, that he delights in her every word. If they had only met in another time, in another place . . . She loves a good *dot dot dot*. And somehow her fantasy man is able to communicate this without wrecking either her marriage or his own.

It's Adultery Lite. It's just enough adultery, but not too much. That is what she wants.

Because if she were to bring this fantasy man out into the real world, she would find that men don't say *I'd like to, but I won't* in any pure, self-sacrificing sense. They say it as predators, as cheaters-to-be; they say it as men who cannot be satisfied with anyone's breasts until old age, as men who are preparing for a lifetime of unfaithfulness, if not with you, then with the next one.

Her desire, then, by definition, cannot be fulfilled, because the object of the desire would be destroyed in the acquisition. If she had him, he would not be worth having. He is a logical impossibility.

And she herself—the happy woman in her fantasy who has her cake and eats it too—is also a mythical creature. She is rehearsing for a role she hasn't fully understood. She is training herself to be an antiheroine, walking the path of ruined lives and motherless children.

Yes, there is a difference between a full-blown affair and an affair conducted entirely in one person's mind. And she would be more culpable, to be sure, to carry out these designs. But if you focus your efforts on developing these undetected mental sins, you will have a sure victory—and you will possibly get the second victory thrown in.

Just remember: when it suits you, encourage her to think that only the mind matters and that she may do what she likes with her body. Then, when it suits, encourage her to think that only the body matters and that she may do what she likes in her mind. By these alternating tacks, you may get her to deliver up both her body and her soul to Our Father Below.

The pleasure she seeks is not exactly physical, but it is pure belly nonetheless. Her "heart" has almost nothing to do with it. It's about pleasure—not love. She's just indulging in a bit of emotional masturbation.

Your girl is one of those who are weak as puppies when it comes to physical or emotional pleasures of the quickest kind. The screen, the flattering glance, the bag of candy are all access points. She can't yet fully imagine stronger pleasures than these, can't imagine what it would take to turn to her same-old husband's company, to a difficult book, to a hard-won meal, ultimately to the Enemy Himself. These are the pleasures that take longer to hit the brain but leave a human creature without a belly ache. Keep her in the dark about how low and obvious a game it really is, these endless questions about whether the man *really is so very attracted to her or not*! Let her keep imagining herself a star-crossed lover instead of a sordid, pathetic, gluttonous Goldilocks, scarfing guiltily away in another person's bowl, chair, and bed.

Sincerely,
Madame Hoaxrot

9

On the Perverse Desire

My dear Hemlock,

Bright girl. I understand—it does seem obvious, indeed it *is* obvious. She ought to see that her desire for this young man's attention will eventually clash with the life she is currently building with her husband. But you're overlooking one of the superpowers of woman: the Perverse Desire, or the Desire for the Impossible. Now is as good a time as any to acquaint yourself with it. You will exploit it for the rest of her life.

Woman is stupendous. She can simultaneously want things—really believe that she *ought* to have things—that are absolutely incompatible with each other. A cosmopolitan life in the city, and the romance of the country; a large family, and a small tidy one; a husband named George who is wise and bookish, and her friend's husband, Jake, who is gregarious and outdoorsy. It might seem like the obvious impossibility of her multitudinous wishes would occur to her, but actually that never needs to happen. She can cling to the illusion for her entire mortal life. (I haven't found the ability as strong in the males, although they do it as well. As I once stated rather aptly in my piece "Human Suffering, Human Rage," MAW Newsletter, 1715 ed.: "Women are very much like men, only more so.")

This capacity is one of the greatest allies we have in our work with women. After all, what are we doing, really, but encouraging them to develop in tandem two Great Conflicting Desires: the desire for His "joy," and the desire for autonomy? We encourage them in their fleshly schizophrenia because we find that the heavenish longings can never be totally killed—and besides, sometimes they help disguise the other pursuits we are helping them to get tangled up in. Thus, they can hope for Heaven and run after Hell; they can desire His presence and fervently wish for His absence; they can desire peace but try to get it without laying down their arms.

These are the ultimate conflicting desires that, if you do your job well, she must never examine and compare. You want her never to lay her desires out next to each other and ask about the *logic* of them. How is it possible to "love" the Enemy but to also resist His presence in her private life and innermost thoughts? To long for the "joy" of having no secrets but to keep drinking on the sly or looking at pornography in secret? To make a run for the Enemy's "freedom" but to continually look back at the city she escaped from?

Perhaps your impulse is to carry her along until her desires are unified on our side, totally aligned with the wishes of Our Father Below. But research has shown us that this sort of victory is much more difficult and no more effective at bringing humans home to us in the end.

The fact is, they are not like us. Their impulse toward the Enemy's "joy" myth is still deeply planted, and their lifespans are often too short for them to reach our state of conglomeration. So why not work with the grain? If the Enemy-oriented desires confuse and comfort your patient as she plows along in pursuit of the opposite ends, what is the harm in it? Why should she know what she is doing, after all? Would we not risk forcing her hand?

Don't imagine that we really WANT a full decision. Not yet. Let her cling to the incompatible things for as long as she will.

Remember this in all your work with the girl. You can help her do this with anything. *I want to live contentedly as the Enemy's servant, but I will complain about most of the life He gave me to live. I want children, but I don't want to give up anything to raise them. I want close friends, but I want relationships to be easy and pain-free. I want to be disciplined, but I don't want to discipline myself.*

And so on, ad infinitum. The perverse desire is strong enough to carry her right into old age. She may find herself on her deathbed, still clinging to desires that are impossible and that make less sense as the years go by. She may be brought to greater degrees of insanity every year. Suicide itself is an incompatible desire (the desire for happiness—once again—meeting and clashing with the desire for relief from pain and responsibility).

Unlike ourselves, you understand, human creatures cannot be truly autonomous. It is one of the great tragedies of their kind that, even in the Rebellion, they will only find more subservience, submission to our own glorious and fanatical race. The sorry bipeds are literally incapable of standing on their own two feet.

Sincerely,
Madame Hoaxrot

10

On Diversifying Her Pleasures

My dear Hemlock,

So she has escaped the trap set at the office; so much the worse for you. If you didn't want her to get a fit of conscience, you shouldn't have pushed her so quickly to imagine the affair actually happening in real life; I told you and I told you. You overstepped—in your glee and zeal you forgot her feminine delicacy. And then, the nauseating scene of confession and renewed intimacy with the husband! Well, you have your reward.

You whine in your letter that it wasn't the imagination plants at all; it was a sermon. So some hotshot in the pulpit thought it was a good idea to call out adultery for ten minutes (thus awakening her conscience, in your assessment) and then to call out the merits of the Enemy Son for thirty (thus, I suppose you mean to imply, awakening her affections)?

Sometimes I wonder, do you really believe the things you write?

Well, let's just test this theory, shall we? *Is* it that her affections were suddenly engaged elsewhere? I've read her report, and I've stood in the room with her long enough to see a bit of what goes on in that head.

If her heart were a pie chart, it would look like this: 40 percent what people might be saying about her, 20 percent plans for a new business or new project or new hobby, 20 percent what she will eat/drink/wear/watch/listen to next, 10 percent babies and children, 9 percent whether her husband is respectable and well-liked and will be able to attract true friends for them both, 1 percent the Enemy's promises of happiness and Heaven.

Even her highest affections are not so high. She loves, not holiness itself, but the idea of holiness. She loves the idea of becoming more respectable, more knowledgeable, more fruitful, more righteous. It's a love of progress, of dignity, of potential, of "growth." She still rarely fixes her thoughts on *Him*. At her best, she is engrossed with the idea of herself being more engrossed with Him.

Do take care that her desires never grow too strong. She desires affirmation, and unless you're careful, that desire may drive her into the thunderous waterfall of His notice. She will get more than she bargained for!

He wants her to want Him, and to want Him *strongly*; remember the parable of the talents. The "wicked" servant's wickedness basically amounted to simple caution! And he was the one who remained safely his own master to the end. The Enemy requires a kind of monomania from them. He wants them to invest everything they own in His pyramid scheme, to seek His face to the exclusion of all else, to trade everything for one single solitary pearl. He wants the sort who will take hold of His garments and hold on like a pit bull or a two-year-old.

Instead of this possessed energy of pathetic need, we would have her do what we ourselves do and reserve the autonomy of *diversification*. Diversification of opinion, of desire, of truths to be tasted and rejected, of small plates to nibble. What if feasts of Lamb alone are not to everybody's liking? Can she not be allowed to love what suits her, depending on the day, the hour?

Her flesh already enjoys tasting things—this dress, that friend, this song, that hobby, this man, that flattering attention from a group of laughing friends, this audience, that book, this identity, that church. She, a woman, reserves the right to change her mind, her identity, her affections, her desires. How does she know what may satisfy her tomorrow? Her changing desires are themselves proof that nothing *could* satisfy for all time. Haven't we tasted enough souls to know this? It's the reason we continue our hunt; our victories must continue, or we languish in that terrible gnawing hunger.

Let her continue her own hunt, and don't worry about her desires being difficult to precisely identify with so long as they are properly diversified. If she shows a tendency toward an increasing preoccupation with He Himself ("What would it be like to *meet* Him? What is He *like*?"), we find distraction to be the most effective tack. Let her remember her other loves and ask herself how she could ever give up jazz, for instance, if she were to find that He is not the kind of being who likes jazz. Would He strip her of herself, after all? It's a fair question.

He pretends to invite her into His own pleasure and joy! But we all know His reservations—to which of us did He ever say "You are my Son, today I have begotten you?" or "I will be to you a father, and you shall be to me a son?" Why, if either humans or demons were to receive pleasure after all, did He command us all to worship HIM alone and then demand our satisfaction in the mindless roles He gives us: the humans as dust-men in charge of dust-gardens, we angels as "winds" and "flames," messengers and courtiers? To which of us did He ever give the scepter of uprightness? And can we ever forget His egotistical choice to anoint the Son with the oil of gladness "beyond his companions"? He is as obsessed with hierarchy as we are, after all!

Your girl must be brought to see this situation for what it really is. We will never be anything to Him but "companions," never anything but handmaids designated for service. Nobody but one will be invited to sit at His right hand and be dominant forever; she must see this in order to see why it will never be a sufficient reward to "enter into His joy."

She wants community and inclusion very much—you must take care that she doesn't connect this desire with His Fellowship. He has invited her to forsake other things in order to one day "enter into the joy of her Master." Take care that she sees the barb in this promise ("your MASTER"). He would master them, and they can never truly be one of the Fellowship, when He reserves the center spots of that Fellowship for His own self. That is the price of admission. Never let her forget that bit—or else her desire to be welcomed in may get the better of her, grow into a kind of obsession.

The problem is that His joy, as He describes it, is entirely in Himself. She can have no part in it, not really. If He finds joy in her, it will still be only because He placed a mirror in her that reflects Himself back to Himself—she must be made to see the impossibility of any real autonomy in such a throne room!

In the meantime, we demons are forever galled by the presence, never totally possible to ignore, of the gloating Enemy Son—He who came and bragged before all of our faces of His eternal intimacy within Himself. "I and the Father are one," He said! "The Father loves the Son and shows Him all that He Himself is doing," He said! "For this reason the Father loves Me," He said, "because I lay down My life that I may take it up again." And He will never let us forget, though we do our best under the circs.

There you have it—what I call the Original Clique.

Sincerely,
Madame Hoaxrot

P.S. I did hear a very amusing little story about you from Glutroot; oh, you have been a naughty thing! I see now why you never answered my question about your last assignment. So you were part of the Pain Orgies? We heard all about it, but I didn't know any of you personally. How simply *awful*! I'd heard something about things getting "out of hand" a few scores ago. Someone told me there was a group that "overdid a bit." But they didn't tell me the extent of it—that you got so sloshed you lost your bearings completely and went deranged! How *horrifying*!

It makes so much sense of your situation now that I've heard the whole story. Why didn't you tell me earlier? I'm always happy to reeducate, and it is so helpful to know why my students needed to be enrolled. You know I'd never share it with a soul! My lips are sealed! (Only I did just mention it to a few of the gals I ran into in the Persian Territories yesterday.)

11

On the Pocket Mirrors

My dear Hemlock,

I spent a refreshing weekend inhabiting a roll of packing tape during my patient's sister's move, making sure the end of the roll was completely invisible to the naked human eye.

Yes, by all means, let us talk about the internet.

We weren't sure about it all when they first brought it out—I remember many panicky memos from headquarters about Enemy communications getting out faster. We were alarmed about how outposts of Enemy activity could exchange resources with calls for help or real-time prayer—and I know it sounds disastrous, put like that. All kinds of light pouring into all kinds of places we had kept safely in shadow for thousands of years. And in the end, some disaster has occurred through the internet. But I believe it has done us more good than harm.

I spoke once before about the vanity we tease out online. We have average women imagining they have "fans" who wait with bated breath to see what they are thinking, eating, wearing, and doing. This strange insulation from reality is, yes, one of the great uses of the internet. We have a world of Narcissuses to snack on these days, and it's been great fun. They carry their pools around in their pockets for easy gazing.

The humor of it is that none of these people think of themselves as vain. If it was a simple glass mirror, they couldn't be brought to spend so much time looking into it. It would be too boring, not to mention embarrassing to be seen doing this in public.

But it's not a simple glass mirror. It's a mirror of the soul; it feeds them what they love. It shows them what they love to read—opinions that match theirs. It shows them what they love to shop for—possessions that reflect their tastes in housewares, clothing, and books. It shows them what their friends think of them, in quantifiable measurements of activity (or ghastly silence!).

The junior tempters get so excited about this vanity stuff (and the sex stuff—obviously the Department of Pornography has had its heyday and continues to celebrate like the unhinged idiots they are). But it's very clear to me what the greatest advantage of the internet has been and will continue to be: victory over Time.

While online, the humans experience an existence that has much in common with our own. They become avatars of themselves, wandering around in an aphysical world, occasionally bumping into avatars of other people to enjoy muted versions of fellowship, discussion, or conflict. They whirl through the ether, stupefied and mostly unguarded. Put simply, the internet disembodies and removes them from Time.

Time, as the Enemy created it, is like a road stretching out in front of them. They can only pass over it on the ground, one foot in front of the other. Sometimes their pace feels quick, and sometimes slow, but they can only pass through the moments singly. When they are working hard, or in pain, their pace feels burdensome. They count every inch, every second. When they are on a pleasurable stretch of road, the time practically skips for them. They look up and say something like, "What, ten o'clock already?" And we know, with a cringing feeling of loss, that they have actually experienced every one of those moments with no skipping, no hitchhiking—and yet enjoyed the feel of them, swum through them, as it were, even though they were trapped in a place and time of HIS choosing!

However, the mirrors in their pockets and on their TV stands do something that only mind-altering substances could do before now.

They lift them right out of time completely.

The Enemy, of course, is outside of time as well. But He's outside of it in a different way; He flies overhead and manages to be in every place and every time simultaneously. To

Him, a thousand years are as a moment because He is simply taking advantage. He plays nasty tricks on us all, dodging about while we are forced to stay on the track of His making, keeping both hands inside the vehicle at all times, as it were. And then in His "above the rules" relationship with time, He always finds a way to work out His own dastardly intentions. He keeps us at a disadvantage in all of this. Let me tell you, if I had a tenth of His abilities, what I could do with them! But He will never share. Some humans have called Him the Lord of Time, but we know that He is actually the Despot of Time. He takes what He wants at every turn.

The humans live in His Time. But some of them find ways to escape it, and in this, they have the opportunity to become more like us.

We are proud to have rejected the tyranny of time, with all its crushing restrictions. You may have noticed one side effect of this: we always seem to be losing a clear sense of WHEN we are. A pleasant haze thickens our sense of time's passing. You know, Hemlock, how you can never quite tell how long it's been since you last experienced a victory, a meal? How you can never quite remember how long it's been since we took our first Great Stand by the side of Our Father Below? How sometimes you feel an unbearable eagerness to escape from the present moment, because of your hunger? But you don't know WHEN you want time to move to?

Some have ventured to say this semi-drunken state is a retaliation from the Enemy. (There was one heretic writer you may have learned about in school; he was rightly removed from the reading lists after he said something about "the unintended obscurities of rebellion"). But for me, I have always seen it as an advantage, a blessing in disguise, a natural result of our freedom from Him. Do we really *want* to know how much time is passing in this war? Do we really *want* to know how long we wait from one meal to the next? Do we really *want* to have our senses sharpened and tuned to the awful anxieties of each defeat, the ear-rattling sounds that escape our notice because we are floating in a relief of cool, dark independence from His Time?

This is what the screen gives the humans. It gives them the same escape. They don't know when or how they came to be on their phones. They only know they are freed from the plodding, repetitive step of moment after moment. The joys and sorrows of life are muted for them, and they are carried down the road of time without knowing or caring.

Give your girl plenty of encouragement to spend her days with the mirror in her pocket. It will only do her good—as much good, I'd say, as a good old-fashioned drug addiction (they work the same way). Her back and neck contract into a hunched position, her mind relaxes, and her feet leave the pavement. She arrives in another place on the road, much further on, bloated in soul, legs atrophied. *See?* You tell her. *You need not deal with the toil.*

Her legs will, indeed, atrophy. The strength it takes to travel through time will simply leave her. In the end, she'll be sitting at a table with friends, and the burden of having her legs touch the road of time will be too much, even at such an easy and pleasant part of the road! She'll pull her phone out of her pocket, and it's not even WORK she's avoiding; it's pleasure.

The advantage for us is that our patients can be brought to the end of a wasted life more gently and easily than ever before. As one of our great contemporaries has said, the best state for man is to be "fuddled," doing neither what he ought nor what he likes. And with that little attention-grabber in her pocket, your patient will slowly learn to "like" fewer and fewer things.

And that will include the Enemy, never forget, not just the Enemy's world!

How's that for a treat! You get to invite her, whenever possible, to live life on the other side with us. And believe me, it won't agree with her as well as it does you . . .

Sincerely,
Madame Hoaxrot

12

On Female Friendship

My dear Hemlock,

It's almost too late to start thinking about the Patient's female friendships. In some ways, kindergarten is the time to really get out ahead of them properly. But there are still some principles that will help you now.

Obviously, these relationships can be quite dangerous. Friendship, as the Enemy intends, is a salve on the weary and painful parts of the rodents' lives. Friendship can lead to an increase in human delight and innocent humor, the easing of human toil, the passing of Enemy propaganda, and the spurring on to what the Enemy calls "love and good deeds."

On the other hand, the human drive to pursue friendship and belonging is also a powerful tool for us. Women evangelize one another—why should they not evangelize for us? Women advise one another—why should they not distract one another with irrelevancies all the day long? Women warn one another—why should they not be busy at our work, stirring up fears about anything and everything except robust (unhealthful) fear of the Enemy?

Your approach will depend somewhat on the personality of the Patient:

Is she naturally independent? Encourage her to keep distance between herself and other women, to never need them more than they need her. Strengthen her impulse to guard herself from the discomfort of anyone "meddling" in her heart's affairs. This will eliminate the worst kind of friend (and, of course, the Enemy Himself, who is the most meddlesome of all).

Is she naturally clingy and emotional? Push her toward a woman she can wrap her whole heart around, thus beginning a good healthy idolization. Encourage many moments of uncertainty about the relationship, and teach her to dwell on the uncertainty. Gradually, you may get her to watch her friend's face with more earnest attention than she ever gave to the Enemy's.

Is she competitive? Regularly introduce the question of superiority—who is "better," herself or her friend? For many patients, we've been able to blur the line quite a bit between hatred and friendship. Even among women who know the

Enemy, the competitive ones often have moments where their desire to dominate their friends completely overwhelms any actual affection they feel for them.

Is she lazy and self-indulgent? Encourage her to stay out of friendships that require effort on her part. (This means she'll be steering clear of all true friendships, but she can be made not to see that.) Put a clear picture in her mind of a friendship she's never had, one that is easy and intimate, with a deep heart connection and a steady stream of fun. This imaginary friendship never requires listening without talking, praying for someone who is in a season of dry prayerlessness, or unrequited service.

Is she given to constant fears about being "left out"? Encourage her to dwell on that. Again, there's an imaginary place she wants to reach, one of security within her circle of friends, one that makes her feel she's arrived. Never allow her to examine this desire in logical terms. Exactly how much friendship would be enough? Who could actually love her with a love that grounds her whole existence? She must never think of *Him*. Keep her eyes on the friends who had lunch without her, and then give her lots of busywork to do, to "make sure it never happens again."

Is she the natural leader of her friends? It is excellent fun to isolate this kind of person inside her charisma; she can be encouraged to treat all her friends like minions or admirers. It will be comfortable for her. But she'll always secretly suspect that her friends are not truly her friends—they don't seem to challenge her so much as bask in her glory. If asked, she would still express a loneliness and longing, and with a little guidance, she can be taught to imagine that this is because the right match in friendship has never found her.

What is the goal, you might ask? Big picture, it's the same as in any other area of life. Your aim is to create distance between your patient and the Enemy. But you want to create distance between the women as well. Even when you're encouraging codependency, it's never true intimacy you want to achieve. It's exploitation. We don't mind women being physically or emotionally close; they can climb all over each other, for all we care. It's a certain kind of like-mindedness we abhor, one in which the creatures co-labor with joy, always within the bounds of Enemy teaching, receiving refreshment and insight for the Enemy's work. This sort of thing creates a destructive bond that could last, quite literally, forever.

In the Enemy's view of friendship, the women reach for Him and get friendship thrown in. Instead, we want these women to reach for friendship and get neither. We want them to turn away from the Enemy toward their friends and, in the end, to find that their friendships are solitary, poor, nasty, brutish, and short.

You certainly don't want her to lay her friendships down at the Enemy's feet and ask Him His bidding in the matter. If they start asking anything along the lines of *whom* He would have them serve or encourage, *what* He would have them say, *how much* intimacy to allow, etc., you will need to immediately move onto the offensive.

Here are three examples of more helpful questions to introduce to her mind:

1. "*Do my friends love me enough?*"

Of course, this is the same question we like her to be asking about her husband or her parents or her siblings. But in those familial relationships, the question tends to cause irritation. In female friendship, the question is more likely to cause anxiety.

We want her to feel that the role of her friends is to validate her existence: "I have friends, therefore I am." Or even more fun: "I have no friends, therefore I am not." This is the thought we thrust upon her whenever someone declines her invitation to dinner, whenever she catches a glimpse of two other women in deep conversation.

It sounds like a stretch, but believe me, it isn't to these overgrown kindergartners. They learned their habits of female interaction in that early age of friendship bracelets and *You can't sit here.*

She will have been told that the Enemy has in some sense "declared" her existence and worth. But it's terribly easy to make the humans forget this. She wakes up many days of her life with the subconscious question *Am I?* And if she attempts to answer this question through her intimacy with other women (or men, for that matter), she'll be on a merry ride for the rest of her life.

As long as you keep her mind on the way she's being treated, you can turn friends into enemies very easily in her mind. Nobody will ever consider her enough, admire her enough, think of her enough. (You might think that, once you get her friends into the category of enemy, it will occur to her that she should approach them the way the Enemy told her to in his Terrible Talk on the Mountain. But I promise she'll never make the connection. "Love your enemies," His nonsensical command, is hard enough when she has a clear enemy. But what about when her "enemy" is just a friend who has forgotten to include her in a text invitation? What about when her "enemy" has slapped her on the cheek by repeating her private prayer request to a third party? What if the person "taking her tunic" is just a lady from church who borrows her Instant Pot and doesn't bring it back?)

Another good question:

2. "*How can we define this relationship?*"

The female creatures love to assign names to their relationships. "This is my boyfriend," "This is my mentor," "This is my best friend." She finds security in these titles because the titles denote exclusive rights and commitment. And in relationships where exclusivity is NOT commanded by the Enemy, we find it very helpful to encourage humans to demand it.

(Of course, in a relationship the Enemy designed to be *exclusive*, we work the other way, bringing in a third party and creating alien *inclusivity*—a lover to fracture a marriage, a major project to distract a parent from their child, etc.)

We want them endlessly gazing at the relationship itself—analyzing it, inspecting it, checking it for integrity. This is much more useful to us than when they start to gaze at *something else*, together. When two women are drawn together by a common interest, be on your guard. It's not that we can't use interests in quilting or books or exercise. Of course there are openings for idolatry and sin in any of these things. But generally speaking, an innocent activity that involves the Enemy's physical realm is much more dangerous to us than not.

At the very least, we like to temper pure enjoyment with side questions: *How do I look when I'm doing this thing? This thing I'm enjoying, do the important or interesting people also like it? If I do this thing, can it carry me up the social ladder?* Nothing is more helplessly nauseating than the sight of these creatures enjoying a thing HE made and recognizing that HE made it. We are on dangerous ground when two of them begin to enjoy one of the Enemy's creations at the same time, side by side. It's Enemy-worship, Hemlock, nothing less.

You must be careful about your patient's connection to the woman named Mary; it has a worrisome tendency. The two of them both love to cook, and they seem to talk about cooking and the Enemy when they're together, almost interchangeably. This is the very thing we do not like.

3. "*Who is the superior in this relationship, her or me?*"

This final question only works with a more competitive personality. The competitive woman will never say this aloud to anyone, least of all her friends. But if you peer into her mind, you'll find that, for each of her female acquaintances, she has a subconscious answer to this question. She fully believes that some of her friends are (slightly) her superior, and that others are (slightly) her inferior.

In this we, as you know, relate to them very well. We also understand hierarchy; don't we know how thoroughly all interactions are ruled by it! (Naturally, you and I are an exception, my dear. I've always considered you my equal in every way!)

Your girl will place some friends in the "superior" category. These are the women she's driven to make a good impression on, to pursue for closer intimacy, or to avoid. Those are truly her only options. She cannot completely ignore the "superior" friend. She'll find that she's incapable of it.

A good example of this dynamic is your patient's friend from work, Rachel. Rachel has been placed firmly in the "superior" category, and she knows it. Though the two go out to lunch together, are both desk workers, and occupy much the same place in society, your patient ceded a position of authority to Rachel when they first met. I understand it's on account of Rachel's good looks and outgoing personality.

You may wonder if this recognition of superiority may backfire, causing a sort of humility in your patient. But it never seems to do so. Humans seem instead to be driven to either groveling or resentment. Apparently, they intuit the principle we all know: in every relationship there must be a dominator and a dominated. (Always excepting you and I, dear!)

Never fear. What you are seeing in your patient is not true humility. When she arranges her day, bending over backward in case Rachel deigns to be available for lunch, she is actually serving her own ends. She believes that mixing with a person she deems "superior" will somehow elevate her; she expects something of Rachel to rub off. She thinks she's doing "Christian fellowship," when actually she's hanging on for dear life, by her thumbs, to the rungs of a social ladder.

This is where we want to keep her.

When your patient places a friend in the "inferior" position, her reaction is quite different but equally positive. Here, she's the one deigning to spend time with the other person. She's the one who feels secure and unruffled when plans are canceled. She's the one who doesn't have to spend time thinking of the other when they're apart. She never replays what was said and plans for their next meeting. All of that sort of thing falls to the "inferior" friend.

Either way, the interactions that result are rarely honest, rarely free, and rarely do anything to promote true intimacy or lasting relationship.

Your friend,
Madame Hoaxrot

13

On Gardening and Babies

My dear Hemlock,

Ah, thank you so much for the mind-numbingly lengthy exposition on your choice of name—fascinating! So hemlock is poisonous, is it? So it has a long history of contribution to human death, does it?

That's all very well. But darling, really now.

Don't you get a rather sick feeling when you stare too long at vegetation? Personally, I can never contemplate the nasty overgrown physical world without disgust and irritation. Even the poisons are entirely too much physicality for me; growth and greenery never did a spirit any good. Smells, seeds, fertilizations, rains, roots, leaves, fruit—how can you bear to look at them, think of them, name them? And to name yourself after anything so verdurous . . . ugh, well. To each his own . . .

I never can identify with the plight of a demon who has frustrated materialistic proclivities. The shock I felt when I witnessed the Early Intermarriages! I simply don't understand what motivates such things—the desire to become one of *them*. Obviously, I've experienced my own fascination with the female. It just seems to me that these maladjusted demons misunderstand the proper way to enjoy her.

No, the material world ought to be below the notice of a truly self-actualized demon. This is my firm opinion, and I wrote as much in my critically acclaimed piece "On the Dangers of Long Walks to Human Persons" (Blackguard Press, 1931).

Which puts me in mind—are you entirely serious in your blithe admission that your girl has gotten into gardening? How cheerfully you tell me about her "harmless" new employment.

Have you ever *seen* a tomato?

Hemlock, dear. Even someone with your particular sort of intellect should not have overlooked something so obvious. Does not the sight of a sugar snap pea, hanging on the vine near its blossoming brethren, fill you with a vague sense of horror and foreboding? This should have been hint enough.

The act of raising something, of nurturing and feeding and protecting it—this is absolutely the Enemy's sort of thing. It reeks of the Enemy. When she plucks the weeds, fights back the encroachment of pestilence and pest, marvels at the addition of new leaves not of her making—what exactly do you think will happen in her disgusting little human soul? Despair? Self-absorption? Indolence? How exactly do you propose to produce any of the cardinal vices in the black dirt of her garden?

No, you have given her over to her humanity, in the worst sense; you have allowed her to enter *His* domain for perhaps half an hour each day, and you've done it without a struggle.

What she calls "losing track of time" in her garden is nearly the opposite of the soul-sucking thing you want to do with her pocket mirror. You want her to float unconsciously above time, to give time to her pocket mirror against her will or awareness; you want the time to simply disappear into the ether, over and over and over, and leave her without refreshment, healthy fatigue, or new knowledge.

But gardening does none of that. Because it's pleasurable, gardening will cause an hour to ease by, but she will be utterly present for every second of it. She will not *lose* the time at all. You will not have stolen anything. She will come to the end of that time with a full awareness of where she has walked, and her soul will be *more* ready for the next stretch of road, not less.

And don't think for a moment she can garden without a pleasant, glowy awareness of the human vermin growing in her belly. Yes, I've heard all about it. So she got knocked up by the man, did she?

This is bad news for you in the same way that the gardening is bad news. Growing a baby and growing a tomato are not totally unalike. She knows she's somehow involved in both processes. She was there when the baby was conceived—a pleasure she participated in, no less!—just as she was there to put the tomato seed into a little tray. But beyond that, she is a strange combination of spectator and participant.

In both, she feels herself to be a witness to miracles. At the moment, she sees the world as both grittily natural and blessedly supernatural. A pregnancy feels natural to her in one sense, because she can see and feel it. But it also feels supernatural, because she can neither see nor hardly imagine the building blocks of new life. The life inside her is both contained by her body and totally beyond her comprehension. As far as she's concerned, it's magic. It's growing, and someday it will speak and think and act, and she will have carried it inside herself, but did she *make* it happen? Not hardly. She knows firmly now; it's happening *to* her much more than *by* her. She's only a vessel, like the dirt she's playing around in.

This kind of thing tends to draw back the curtain on the world we have tried to camouflage from the humans for the last several hundred years. We ourselves are never allowed to forget that the physical and spiritual realms are both quite real and terribly, terribly intertwined. But we have had great success in making them unaware of it.

Through the foresight of some of our greatest tactical giants, we have led them to believe, in a kind of mass hypnosis, that "science" (by which they mean anything observable and repeatable) is the only real thing. The "natural" operations of seasons, flora, fauna, human invention, sleeping, waking, eating, etc. are taken at face value. But anything they call "supernatural," including even dearly held spiritual beliefs, they have come to regard as *not quite real*. Thus, every "normal" physical thing is regarded as totally trustworthy, safe, and self-ordering. But the unseen—and this includes the spirit world, the afterlife, the moral law, and the Enemy Himself—is constantly relegated to questionable status.

Unfortunately, when a woman like this feels a baby kicking in her womb, she might question the tenuous logic of her latent materialism. If something must be observable and repeatable to be "real," what about this being inside her, which she knows in the marrow of her bones to be a new SOUL, and which wasn't there a few weeks ago, and which neither she nor anyone else can repeat or, at present, even observe? It smells of magic, and thus of miracles, and thus of the spiritual realm.

From there she may come to notice the same inexplicable tendency in other natural processes. She will realize that a seed that germinates underground is observable and repeatable in one sense, but is also caused by something that no self-aware scientist can explain. Anyone can say *what* a seed does. But *why* does it do it? And *how*? What is the unapproachable mystery occurring in the darkness under the dirt? What if the world isn't very safe at all, and what if nothing is really observable and repeatable in the sterile and contained sense she's always meant it? What then?

So here you have a really deplorable situation in which her mind is constantly drawn back to the "supernatural," and from there, to Him, every time there's another ghastly fluttering inside her or another wave of sickness, every time another leaf buds. She is absolutely alight with the awareness.

You sit, looking on like a kindly grandmother as the beasts mate and mess about with seeds. What exactly do you think all this horrible, dirty, fleshful activity leads to? Nothing short of joy, you silly ass. And to add insult to injury, now we have another tomato! Another human! Where does all of the Enemy's get-up-and-go come from, really? His own self? Or does He do it simply to taunt us?

I have no doubt of His malicious enjoyment in our suffering.

Keep your head on straight, "Hemlock,"
Madame Hoaxrot

14

On Raising a "Strong Woman"

My dear Hemlock,

So your patient is having a girl—another victim for the spit. It's a scene I've watched many times before, and I can picture it now:

Your patient leaves the ultrasound appointment and walks aimlessly through a mall nearby. Her mind is reeling. She realizes suddenly that she'd been hoping for a boy; somehow it would have been simpler. As she walks unseeingly through racks of clothes and purses, her imagination is full of the difficulties that lie ahead. What will her daughter struggle with? What will people do to her? How can she protect this little girl from the inevitable hardships and pains of life?

After a few hours of these thoughts, she resolves to raise a "strong woman" and to be a stronger woman herself in order to be an example to her daughter. She is only slightly comforted by this resolution.

Well. Don't let this sort of language alarm *you*, at any rate.

All of the humans like to make brash statements about raising strong women and being strong women themselves, but few of them know what they mean by it. They might have vague ideas mashed together from images of a taekwondo girl in heels, an intelligent girl in glasses, or a girl who likes to march in rallies. "Strength," you see, is anything to anyone and nothing to nobody; it is a meaningless word, like "education" or "love."

Your patient is perhaps not perfectly clear about the kind of woman she intends to raise, but you can be perfectly clear about your own goals, both for your patient and for the new creature.

Let me tell you the kind of strong we want. We want a cold, metallic center running right down the middle of our women in place of a living spine. We want the pain of life—the pain of being sinned against since childhood, the pain of sinning and being unable to stop, the pain of sickness and death and hunger—to melt her, right down in the middle of her soul, and then we want that melted place to harden up into a steel core.

The Patient is quite right. Her daughter will suffer, just as she herself has suffered. You want the Patient's suffering to increasingly produce only bitterness. Seeing her daughter's upcoming suffering will be a prime opportunity to produce a bumper crop. This in turn will make work easy for the daughter's caseworker in later years. Women usually learn their style of suffering from their mothers, whether they're aware of it or not. If you teach your patient to choose bitterness in the face of hardship, it doesn't matter what form that bitterness takes. It may look like querulous, nervous hand-wringing or hard-as-nails, nobody's-fool bristles. But rest assured, the daughter will pick it up. She will learn it like a lesson. So if you teach the mother to settle into the habits of bitterness, both you and some lucky future co-tempter will benefit.

The resolve that comes from bitterness is never a dangerous form of resolve. It will never lead her to do anything threatening to our kind. Rather, it is a seat of absolute resistance to the will of the Enemy, and it will manifest in a variety of lines drawn in the sand of her life: *Thus I will do, and no more*, she will say. *Here I will go, and no further.*

"My husband has failed to love me well. Never again will I willingly go to bed with him."

"Never will I stop doing what's best for my mental health." (Which could easily be made to include overspending on self-care, dumping her husband, abandoning her parent to the nursing home and her child to the state, etc.)

"Never will I get a job to help with the finances, no matter what my husband asks."

"Never again will I walk through the doors of a church."

"Never will I forgive my father, my boss, my sister, etc."

"Never will I stop grieving my lost child, job, home, spouse, childhood, youth, etc."

She is capable of harboring this steel pill of resolve into infinity (literally). It is her attempt to eradicate future pain, to demonstrate to the Enemy that she isn't going to be taken in again.

To help her forge this steel spine, you'll want to begin by encouraging her in long episodes of worry. Worry is fixated on the future and inspired by the past, and it does very good work ruining the present. All worry is good worry.

So as she imagines this infant female's life, encourage her to think of all possible issues very quickly, in rapid succession, like a womanhood "worst of" compilation. Acned skin, frizzy hair, hips that are too narrow or too wide. Women's magazine models with photoshopped faces. Myriad unfulfilled feminine longings. A world of men who won't commit, men who refuse to lead, men who leave, men who hit, men who support the mill of pornography and trafficking. Remind her of the most difficult parts of marriage—its frustrations and risks, boredom and heartbreak. Call to mind the emotional burdens inevitably coming to the female creature's body: girlish pouts and early-life menstruation and late-life menopause.

Then encourage her to try to think her way around these difficulties, for herself, and on behalf of her daughter. Encourage her to imagine white-knuckle ways of simply "deciding" not to allow these sorts of things. *Do not trust a man. Do not care about societal beauty standards. Do not want the things you are supposed to want! Be different enough to not have to deal with the things women must deal with!* That is where the steel spine resolve comes in. She wants to avoid pain; we should not mind helping her to do so. (Of course, she will have to experience a kind of torment later, in the time of her transmortification, but she doesn't need to think about that yet.)

The Enemy, in the meantime, has another kind of strong woman in mind.

The strength she forges for herself (with our help) is designed to protect her from pain, or at least to help her make angry protests against pain that she cannot avoid. The strength He forges for her is designed to protect her from the world, the flesh, and . . . well, you know.

First, He begins by disarming her completely. Then He puts what He calls a "heart of flesh" into her (nasty metaphor).

This heart of flesh behaves very differently from the steel backbone of bitterness. It doesn't protect her from pain at all, or indeed from sickness, loss, and even death (she must lose her life "in order to gain it," He insistently tells them). But the new heart tends to make her strangely and illogically unmoved by fearful things, even imminent dangers we point out to her. The heart also leaves her ears open to certain parties in the Enemy's camp, but it makes her increasingly deaf to the most sensible worldly voices.

When He gets His hands on her, she will slowly transform into something you will shudder to witness. And although

He won't allow her the self-made steel spine, if she lives long enough, He will begin to make her another kind of spine to go with her new heart. This will be a living spine, something that becomes increasingly strong but supple, flexible and resilient. (You will wonder: how can a will be both strong and yet flexible? It's a material we haven't gotten a good reading on yet—not like the metal we understand, but something else. Research is growing very close to back-engineering the substance, however, and we will shortly have what we need to dismantle this kind of a spine on contact.) The female creature who is long in the Enemy's house begins to be able to push things forward, to accomplish things, to overwhelm long-established outposts of our people in a uniquely female style.

How does she work? As I said, there are some parts that remain veiled in shadow for us. We only know that she is an enemy who achieves her victories by softening and then enveloping her prey (much like those spiders whose venom liquidates a victim's insides). She draws a nice bath for her children and then tells them a Bible story; she forgives her husband quietly, setting the stage for his soft underbelly to accept the barbs of Enemy arrows; she brings her neighbor a meal and then offers Enemy propaganda in response to the first big emergency. She seems to work by moving things gently forward or by filling things out—behaving more like a vine or a running stream than like your more conventional and efficient object, the battering ram.

So you see, the backbone of her own making will be much better for our cause, and you must get in at this moment of raw feeling. She must begin her resolutions, if not for herself, than for the sake of her little darling *in utero*.

Surely you will have seen that all those resolutions I mentioned earlier—*I won't forgive, I won't let go of this prized possession, I won't resist this trait that is central to my personality*—are just seed forms of the Great Resolve. We ourselves constantly carry the same resolve made of the same metal.

One of my favorite patients of all time was a wonderful example of this. I was somewhat taken with her, really—admired her, one might say. She's the reason I go by "Madame" now. Eighteenth-century French culture was rather the good old days for me.

This madame of mine was the queen of the room in any room. She ran one of the famous *salons* of Paris, where artists and thinkers gathered to slosh around in gorgeous lines of thought, many of them produced by ourselves and fed into their ears in long woven strands. On my lead she gave such lovely speeches about the strength of women, about the rejection of the procreative and the domestic, about the new days to come when women would decide matters of state while men ran schools and daycares and public eating places. The men laughed at her and petted her, and she carried on affairs with them, although she could see they didn't take any of it seriously and only enjoyed hearing her whisper violent words in her boudoir, about the destruction of the monarchy and the overthrowing of their enemies.

She was a strong woman, indeed! The fire of a thousand suns was in her heart, in her resolve never to bend her neck under any conventional yoke, even as she bent her body and mind in service of a new lover or philosopher's leading. She was immovable when it came to the tugging needs of her small children (born without her consent or desire!), absolutely stone when it came to the broken pleadings of a woman whose husband had been led away into her embrace!

We were all a bit shocked the day the mob broke into her château at Versailles and dragged her to the guillotine; she as much as anyone.

We all had a taste of the *femme forte*'s torment that day. She was delicious. I still visit her now and then. She keeps her steel center, even now! I told you before—a female soul is really something.

Sincerely,
Madame Hoaxrot

15

On the New Mother

My dear Hemlock,

Well, here we are. We knew this day would come. She has pushed a human creature through her body and right out into the air, gasping, wriggling, and pink. Nasty, freakish little worm.

It looks like a little pig wrapped in white blankets, but you can already tell it's one of them. It has that little stamp of the Enemy's making, "forever" branded right across its eyes.

After a few days basking in the wonder of their little evidence of copulation, letting nurses show them how it works, they've been unceremoniously discharged from the hospital.

They strapped their little creature in a back seat and drove very carefully home.

And now some new work can begin.

For the next several months, your patient will feel physically not herself. There is something in her body that always fluctuates but, now, in this season, will drop off very suddenly and leave her in the lurch. It is part of the curse their kind Heavenly Father placed on their mother Eve.

The humans call it "hormones"—we call it "opportunity." It is perfectly physical and constitutes a real testing for her. She may not expect this. And her delirious love for the child will be so mixed together with the emotional roller coaster of her physical ailment that she may never know which is which. The important thing is to fill her mind with the belief that everything she thinks and feels is quite rational. Discourage any humorous willingness to laugh at herself, at the outrageous pressure she is under, at the sleeplessness and the physical pain and the rest of it. Encourage her to take herself very seriously, along with all the irrational thoughts and indignities of postpartum life.

Also, exacerbate the sufferer's typical belief that their suffering will last forever. Any human being who suffers physically is vulnerable to this message. "You are hurting now—and you will always hurt in this way." "This thing is difficult to do now; you will have to keep doing it the same way forever."

The Enemy is always trying to bring the creatures back to just the one moment, just the one day, just the one afternoon.

He tells them to ask for their "daily" bread. He wants them to trust Him for the very air in their lungs and the clothes on their backs, and His intangible aid is usually sent in ration packets that are frequent but small. Oppose Him by encouraging her to try to hoard the rations of help in preparation for an eternity of this same suffering.

There are also some helpful marital habits we can start on right away.

In the early days, you must encourage her to exclude all considerations, including her husband, in her myopic love for her child. This will be easy to accomplish. Every cell in her body is calling out for her baby—she is religiously devoted to its every sound, every movement. None of the cells in her body call out for her husband, not now. She must be encouraged, as the months tick by, to surrender entirely to this impulse and to consider it just, to be surprised and even outraged at the idea that her husband might desire her time or attention.

This will be easy to connect to another useful tendency—her belief in her husband's utter incompetence when it comes to babies. And he *is* probably incompetent; at least, his incompetence probably outpaces hers. However, the disparity in their self-confidence is still greater. She believes she knows more than she really does; he believes he knows less than he really does. Encourage her in this delusion, and feed her new ways to communicate it: a snort of laughter at his "mistake" in the method of offering a bottle, a condescending direction in the administration of a diaper, an absolute refusal to hear his suggestions about letting the child cry instead of picking it up instantly.

You might even encourage her to pit father against child a bit. She will resent her husband for asking anything more of her when she's already pouring so much energy into the child's needy little mouth. She will make him feel rather guilty for wanting anything from her in the way of service, conversation, or physical interaction. They will both begin to take her exhaustion and inaccessibility as a matter of course.

These are the seeds we use later on to discourage the father from taking an active role in training and teaching the child. We aim to produce a weed of true incompetence and passivity on his part, the kind that will make her utterly despair of him in years to come. She won't see that she set the stage for his passivity by giving into her driving instinct to hover and care for the child and ignore his input.

Many of the new-mother phenomena are beyond your control and perhaps beneath your notice—sickness and sleep, bizarre episodes of hand-wringing and equally bizarre episodes of tearful gratitude—all more or less inevitable in this heightened state. The fact is, a newborn child is always a blow. It reminds us of the fact that they multiply, they spread like rabbits, and He keeps filling His halls of Heaven with them as the years go by. He has passed us right over; that's the long and short of it. Ever since the first creature in the garden, He has always seemed to think of *them* first. Never mind little old us, serving Him for millennia without complaint! But who did He go and place the Image upon? The two-leggers.

Purely spirit we remain, and proud to be so! Down with the hairy little beggars.

Sincerely,
Madame Hoaxrot

16
On Parenting

My dear Hemlock,

Now that the woman is embarking on her parenting journey, it's time for you to embark on a little journey of your own. This is a new stage of the game. You will begin by carefully reading through the latest edition of my pamphlet, "Tempters in the Charge of Humans in the Charge of Children." You'll find it terribly instructive and widely applicable for future cases. But I write today to give you additional notes, specific to the American parent and the work we've done on their views of authority. We've had enormous success in the last few decades with very little effort. Well, if not little effort, narrow effort. A concentrated attack on authority gives us victory on so many other fronts. This is the work I want you to build on. So let me set down the method for you, beginning with some basics.

Human children, first of all, need authority in order to thrive. The Enemy creates them in this weaselly condition. Obviously He intends to use it for their ultimate subordination to Himself (I touched on this some years ago in our conversation about the perverse desire).

However, it gets complicated, because they're also born with an innate desire for something we might call "happiness." The advantage is that none of them are born with a clear sense of what will make them happy, and their blind quest for happiness often collides with what is "good" and "true." The Enemy's book repeatedly admits the impossible position human cubs are in from birth: "Folly is bound up in the heart of a child," says the proverb. In other words, the Enemy admits that He spits them out into the world with no sense at all and then punishes them for seeking the only end they are born capable of pursuing. If your patient can't see the question in that statement, do help her find it . . .

So human children are born with two conflicting forces at work: the need for authority, and the desire for happiness. The Enemy has done nothing to reconcile these two opposing forces. He has made it strictly logical, coldly unstoppable; He does nothing to fudge the numbers for them, to make reality even just a little bendy to allow for their own perceived needs.

You see the way before you.

The Enemy has given parents the responsibility of demonstrating the order of His universe through their authority. You obviously will attempt to use the parent as an agent of our own Father's Chaos instead. The "happiness" the cub pursues will be confused and mottled by sin from a very early age—all you must do is get the parent to repeatedly choose to submit to the child's confused pursuit of happiness.

This is a very simple operation to perform on the American mother of the moment. Her friends and almost every "expert" voice are with you. Also on your side is her own personality. Your patient may affirm the idea of authority in the abstract, but she's naturally averse to playing the role of authority figure. She doesn't *want* to wear this mantle. Her husband doesn't much want to wear it, either. Most of the adults they know share this aversion.

And how the children do suffer!

You may witness it at leisure if you but take a stroll through the country on a sightseeing tour. Babies slapping their mothers in the face and being told in words much too long for them to understand why it "isn't polite to be so unkind to Mommy." Three-year-olds, the terror of the nursery, being given their choice of this shirt or that shirt, this meal or that meal, this time-out or that loss of screen time. Eight-year-olds telling their parents that what they do with their phones is "none of your business" and being proudly given a choice of educational methods, of parental custody arrangements, of whether to keep to their rooms and play video games or sit with the family at supper. Fourteen-year-olds, who haven't heard a word their parents have said since the age of two, utterly at the mercy of their phone and Adderall and despair. Parents standing helplessly by, wringing their hands and asking the family doctor for some kind of sign.

It's a wonderful time to be alive, Hemlock!

Your patient is so new to the process; she would look at any of these children and see them as utterly outside the realm of possibility for her family. Her own sweet girl is a darling in diapers, and she is confident the darling will always be darling. Already, she leans into her own passivity.

At this point, it's easy for her to give way to the love of her life, her little daughter. She doesn't *mind* doing more or less whatever her child wants—and besides, her child usually wants to do delightful things. Mama doesn't yet see the urgent need to practice making commands and enforcing them. For now, it's just so *easy* to arrange life around her child's wishes.

But witness the pain when another child comes along, and her two darlings begin to find each other's wishes inconvenient. She will be nonplussed. She'd be happy to give way to either child—but which should it be? And so she will begin the difficult process of finding work-arounds. Bribe the one child to let go of the other child's toy. Say "maybe" when they both ask for different things. Ask the children leading questions instead of commands ("Wouldn't it be better to play at the park *after* we take our walk?" instead of "No, we're going to walk before we play," and "How would you feel if somebody hit you?" instead of "You'll have to get a spanking for hitting your sister"). You'll want to help her develop new and creative ways of avoiding commands in the first place.

She'll be increasingly shocked at the sheer amount of trouble and work required of her. Over time, resentment will grow. She will soon find that she prefers to ignore her children and look at her phone, or to make one more threat, and then another. This, of course, will make things harder for her the next time around. She'll fall into a settled habit of giving meaningless commands, helpless vindictive speeches, wordy diatribes against bad attitudes. Her words will become cheaper, and little ears will get more deaf. It's a perfect cycle of frustration.

As I said, the level of cultural unity on the subject of authority is unprecedented. For every one friend your patient has who seeks to establish authority in the home, twenty more are busy online undermining the very concept of authority. There are now a million voices using labels like "gentle parenting" or "child-led parenting" to describe something like anarchy.

Children, according to most of the voices your patient hears, should be given free rein to express their emotions in any way that feels natural (read: they should be able to throw tantrums without the mercy of intervention from a calm parent). Children, according to these voices, have the right to make their own decisions (read: they are given many options before they are old enough to recognize anything but their most impulsive desires). Children, according to these voices, should never be arrested in the process of discovering themselves (read: they are left to the impossible task of generating their own virtue).

Thus you have a sea of adults on the internet, earnestly defending a system that has left generations of children alone in a terrifying, limitless, formless reality. We will soon have a world run by foundlings, orphaned by the abdication of authority.

Even among the voices of the church, we've set up a false dichotomy for them, with borrowed language from the tenets of their faith. "Grace" vs. "law," two words we have taught them to pit against each other in their treatment of the Enemy's book, we have now got mixed up in the world of parenting to great effect. Which is better? To "show grace" to your children by letting them ignore your commands, or to "apply the law" by expecting obedience from them when you yourself—never forget, parent—you yourself are a messy Christian who cannot keep the law for even one day!

Many of them can't see the Enemy's law as being written for their good, only as an impossible standard sent to show them their weakness. They will pass on this confused view of authority to their children. *My word is not law at all. My words for you carry no weight and can be safely ignored. I am more concerned with your heart being in the right place than with you "listening" and "obeying."* In this view, the parents are not allowed to fulfill multiple functions of love, joy, teaching, encouragement, admonishment, and loving discipline. The parents are only present so that they can admit their own faults to the child, and so they can mention the Enemy Son to the child whenever he disobeys.

Your patient believes she really wants to "love" her children. Don't allow her to ask what the Enemy might have her do to demonstrate that love. Don't let her see how much peace and joy and tranquility will be in her home if she applies herself to the uncomfortable task of establishing authority.

Eventually, without the benefits of loving correction, her children may become the sorts of people who are difficult for even a mother to love.

Sincerely,
Madame Hoaxrot

17

On the Abstention Bias

My dear Hemlock,

So you've finally noticed your girl is prone to asceticism, and you wonder if anything can be made of it. You certainly took enough time noticing. What we have here is a strong case of the abstention bias, which is the human assumption that *to abstain from something is always the most virtuous choice.* In your patient's mind, the burden of proof is irresistibly thrown onto the side of permissiveness. She feels in her marrow that it must be holier NOT to do something than to do it.

Many of her friends share this bias, which makes it a social tool for us, not just a private one. Let's say the girl is among friends. One of them declares she no longer touches some category of food—processed meats, dairy, gluten, sugar, etc. These days, the woman's stated reason is usually not explicitly spiritual. It is rather an argument about health: the body was not meant to consume the food in question, the food in question is the cause of all societal ills and rising healthcare costs, the food in question has never been consumed in its current adulterated state, etc. etc.

The others listen politely, but soon they find themselves on the defensive. They are suddenly driven to explain, to themselves and to the others, why they still partake of (and recklessly feed to their children!) the food in question.

You will surely have noticed a familiar ring to this conversation. It bears a passing resemblance to one of the classic doctrines: Do Not Taste, Do Not Handle, Do Not Touch. Though today's woman does not often use spiritual language to justify her desire to abstain from certain foods, never doubt that it is a mission of purity. And the abstention bias ensures that when her friend tells her the path to purity and good health is to abstain completely from certain foods, her first instinct is to believe.

Of course, you need not concern yourself with who is right (if any of them are). Whether less sugar and fat helps her physical body is no object of yours. Never stoop to asking such fleshy questions.

What you want to do is leverage the abstention bias to cause her to bind her conscience in areas the Enemy does not care about and to loose her conscience in other areas the

Enemy has declared vitally important. He apparently cares quite a bit about her behavior toward others with differing convictions, her submission to the husband if he happens to have different dietary preferences, and her gratitude as she lives in a world of plenty. You must teach her to forget all of these considerations, to put them in the back seat and let the abstention bias drive the bus.

Your job is to keep her alternating between the guilt and self-righteousness of using flesh to fight flesh. If she chooses not to partake of something, will she be self-satisfied and superior toward those who do? If she does partake, will she be defeated, ashamed, and wallowing in guilt? Fill her mind with questions of calories and macros and GMOs so that her children see her visibly tighten into a coil around mealtimes, and her husband finds his plate increasingly served with a side order of prohibition and raised eyebrows.

Food is one of the best areas of use for the abstention bias. But it is by no means the only one. Remember, when she hears her friends make *any* statement about something their family doesn't do—"We don't watch TV," "We don't celebrate [holiday]," "We don't wear makeup," "We don't use plastic," etc.—she will have to contend with her first impulse toward abstention before she's even able to assess the policy or the reasons behind it.

At minimum, you can use this to get her into some very silly social situations. At maximum, you can use it to develop her into a royal terror of virtue signals and misplaced guilt.

We believe that the reason this bias is common among women is because Eve's blood flows in their veins. Your woman still remembers that lady's first infraction, with the ancestral memory that cannot be analyzed. She remembers that her great error was to partake when she should have abstained.

But you want your patient to overlook the true nature of the infraction—just as Eve did on that glorious day of victory. It was always a twofold command. In the Enemy's confused way of thinking, it was not only a question of abstaining; it was a question of "loving" the Enemy BY abstaining. Eve was to turn *away* from the fruit *toward* the one who made it. Your patient has forgotten the permissiveness of that whole putrid garden. She thinks only of Eve's act of commission, when her first disobedience was really an act of omission *by* commission.

At the end of the day, we want men and women to forbid marriage, to require abstinence from anything at all that the Enemy gave to be received "with thanksgiving." Above all, we want them to forget *His* bias in favor of the goodness of matter, to forget how to receive anything with thanksgiving and prayer. You must see the catastrophic risk of it all becoming holy for them!

An abominable freedom is experienced by a creature who is part spirit and part body and who lives in the pleasure of his body within the bounds set by the Enemy Spirit!

Take care she keeps her eyes on the ground.

Sincerely,
Madame Hoaxrot

18

On Sex

My dear Hemlock,

I recently remembered an old promise that I would give you some pointers for producing sexlessness in your patient's marriage. Now is as good a time as any to try some of these maneuvers. First, a bit of information, in case this whole institution is as mystifying to you as it has often been to me:

Human sexuality is really just a kind of recreation, a natural release of the burden of thought and toil. It is one of those really unfortunate activities I've mentioned before that carries them out of themselves and causes the road of time to move by easily. Indeed, the most buttoned-up churchwomen and churchmen become positively undignified in these private moments.

It can also become a kind of mutual marital hobby, like a totally engaging game of tennis. It seems to function a little bit like the stuff called "butter" they use in their cooking—it bathes all the other surrounding ingredients with flavor and unction.

It is play, but it is a serious sort of play. The man and the woman open themselves up to nearly total vulnerability in these moments. And perhaps worst of all, the Enemy has designated this kind of play as the only way the humans may beget progeny. It's a kind of malicious prank on His part, to imbue something that appears to be purely indulgent with such serious consequence.

Given the Enemy's position, we try to sex-proof a marriage whenever possible. Here are the most up-to-date methods:

1. *Discourage her from accepting sex as a marital duty actually commanded by the Enemy—and if she insists on treating it as a duty, see that she takes no personal pleasure in it.*

The strangest thing is that sex is one of the only activities the Enemy actually *commands couples to regularly engage in*. He doesn't command them to play chess together, or to watch television. But he does tell them not to neglect one another's "conjugal rights."

You want her to evade this command by not thinking much about it. It's rather simple. If she saw it as a clear command and focused her mind on it for a moment, she'd have to wrestle with the question of why: *Why would the Enemy prioritize such a thing? What sort of being is He anyway?* And she'd have to ask herself seriously whether she was obeying the command. *Do not deprive one another? What does that mean for me?*

I don't see why you couldn't accomplish this with your girl. She's as busy as the next woman. And her husband will never bring it up in such a brusque way, even if he's quite aware that the command is being sidestepped.

If you do lose the point when it comes to her withholding—if someone gets to her with the idea of marital "duty"—go after her own enjoyment. Try to convince her that, for a wife, sex is *merely* a duty. This will counteract a great deal of the harmful effect. She must begin to see sex as being invented solely for her husband's pleasure, not her own—a purely giving act. Then you can help her come up with ulterior motives for "giving" in this sacrificial way. Perhaps she wants to build up some power and merit that he must repay. Or perhaps she wants to manipulate him by withholding when he displeases her. Or you may encourage her to give out of fear in order to prevent him from pursuing another sexual outlet.

Make this duty a weight and a burden, not a delight or—Hell preserve us!—something that brings lightness and joviality to the rest of their interactions. Make sure it is on her list of things to do that she already can't keep up with.

More and more, she will begin to simply "clock in" for sex. She will show up only to be a passive participant, which will not only kill her own desire but also kill any sense he has that he can please her. Her husband will know, you see, that she is not fully engaged. Being what he is, he will still show up for these sessions, but he will know he's being cheated out of the most potent form of the institution, which is *mutual* delight. In fact, through the Enemy's backward design, the man experiences the most hazardous effects of physical intimacy through the knowledge of *giving* delight. Get her to ignore this, and you can trick her into giving her halfmost in the full belief that she is doing her duty by him.

Over time, they will each be increasingly frustrated that the other doesn't seem to be fully engaged. With luck, they will perhaps even quit the practice entirely and subside into a kind of sexless roommate relationship, each citing the other's lack of interest.

If you do see her sliding into a state of desire for her own husband, you might try suggesting that the marriage bed is boringly "not naughty enough." Remember, humans are often quite aware that only wrong things can be really fun. Get her to recall the sexual impulses and experiences she had in single life and find that the spark of *wrongness* is now missing because of the Enemy endorsement. (And how well we know the insipidity of missing Wrongness!)

If that fails, you might try the suggestion that sex is really *too* naughty for a respectable woman to enjoy! Remember the principle of Misplaced Shame: just as we encourage the humans to suppress shame over unlawful acts, you must do your best to create shame over acts that the Enemy has declared quite lawful. It may help you here to hearken back to any garbled messages she received in childhood.

2. *Encourage her to dispense sex as if it were a precious (i.e., scarce) commodity.*

If she were single, of course, we would encourage her to give her body away as freely as possible. We have had much success in getting men to see sex as a sort of "right" when they give women something like dinner and a movie. But now that her husband has given her a house, children, and a lifetime commitment, this is the time to teach her to really start counting and stacking her sexual favors. She doesn't want to give away the store, after all!

Get her to deny him pleasant things just for the sake of increasing their value. She must develop the self-assured stinginess of a woman who believes she can instill some kind of discipline in her man by cutting him off from pleasures that are in her power to grant. You want her to withhold sex from him the same way she withholds praise or fried chicken. Otherwise, you live in imminent danger of sex becoming one of the more effective ways that she pours blessing on her husband's head, like the accursed woman in the proverb "who does him good and not harm all the days of his life." This kind of senseless spendthrifting is exactly what you want to prevent in a woman.

She must count, dispense, and protect her resources carefully. You want her to see how dangerous it is to start simply giving away her most valuable assets without bringing any kind of material return on them. What if he were to get used to it? He'd take her for all she's worth.

3. *Teach her to put her husband's sexual needs in a totally different category from other human needs.*

She has a son now. So she knows with mother instinct that if she were to cut her little toddler off from physical contact, to turn away from him in scorn when he reached for her, it would be a kind of cruelty.

You must be very careful that she never makes a connection between the boy's need and the grown man's. They are so different, after all! The boy is all innocence, all helplessness. But if she could look into the heart of her hairy, blustery, sometimes rude husband—the one she has vaguely committed to "honor and obey"—she would see a boy in short pants, a tousle-haired adventurer who needs her touch every bit as much as the son in her lap.

The man is harder to love and more complicated (because, of course, the sexual need is mixed up in a need for respect, and because it has been adulterated at times by sin). So it should be easy work to disconnect the idea of "cruelty" from her cutting him off. He is a grown man! His "sex-mania" has nothing to do with a toddler's need to be held!

You must also keep her from seeing the parallel between her withholding physical intimacy and him withholding, say, conversation, or eye contact. I know of a man who, in a unique and creative form of torture, refused to speak to his wife at all for weeks at a time. He understood the insidious nature of this tactic—active beatings would have been less cruel. (They would also have been more actionable on the part of the church or the law.) Your patient would point to that man and say that this was wicked and controlling behavior. But to withhold marital relations—you want her to think *that* is quite a different thing.

Do also take care that she puts his struggle with lust in a totally different category from her own sin. You want her to see him as an alien creature, or as a failed man. She struggles with bitterness, for instance, but she must see his struggle with pornography as quite a different thing, something only a very wicked person could deal with. She must dehumanize the struggle—and dehumanize the man in the struggle.

Keep her mind on the affront to her own honor and vanity. She is hurt by the fact that her husband would ever even *want* to look at another woman. Let her think of it not as a matter of his spiritual health being threatened but as a matter of insult to herself. This is a great opportunity for her to start withholding from him in order to "improve" or "help" him.

You certainly never want her to read the verses about love "bearing, believing, hoping, enduring, being a perfect doormat in all things"—that is a paraphrase but very nearly right, I think—and to think about what the Enemy might want her to do with these verses when she is feeling hurt.

Sincerely,
Madame Hoaxrot

19

On Wine Night

My dear Hemlock,

Passed a pleasant morning putting one single crayon into each of the dryers of all the women in my patient's neighborhood. It refreshed my mind, and I have read with pleasure your report on the Patient's recent reconnection with old friends from school. A standing engagement for "gals' night" is a perfect setup for the kind of intimacy you want her to have with this group.

You say that they used to call themselves Christians in college, as the Patient herself used to claim in those days, but that they are all insincere, flippant, and slightly jaded mothers now. You seem to think some kind of "drifting" is the goal, as it certainly is, but I hope you don't imagine this drifting will go in the right direction without a little nudging.

The danger for your patient is that she's now thoroughly ensconced in her church community. She has a few relationships there of the dangerous kind, and one or two of them have real influence over her. These are people she respects, desires respect from, and wants to emulate.

So I think you should begin by rubbing, irritating, and inflaming the area of her heart that is most sensitive to inequalities. She is already on a trip wire of injured dignity; she still feels a rough combination of attraction and dread when she spends time with these Christians. She is always divided between her desire to enter into their world and her desire to avoid the pain of insulted pride. And insult her they will. Their very existence is an insult. She can't help but see her flaws in the mirror of their eyes; kind as they are, they show her things about herself that she can't accept without a mad struggle.

If you inflame the felt inferiority, she will withdraw from her church relationships, and this will set the stage for her to throw in with these other, better connections.

We are the misfits, she will begin to say to herself. *We are the ones who really understand how hard life is. We get it.*

These new friends don't make her feel inferior at all. Rather, she indulges herself in a comfortable feeling of superiority when she's with them. Here, at last, she is the wisest in the room! Here, at least, she is self-controlled and self-possessed, because she stops just short of insulting and poking fun at her spouse and children as they do, because she has one fewer glass of the wine, because she abstains from watching some of the shows they watch, because she doesn't believe in abortion, or homosexual practices, or whatever else. (Just make sure there are still a few things that she doesn't agree to; it makes her feel she's "holding the line" in some sense.)

Though she may walk in the same path and sit in the same seat as these scoffers, she'll be awash in the feeling of soothed pride as long as she stays a few steps behind them—they are further down the road than she would ever think of going!

It helps that these ladies laugh a lot—I believe you said that loud laughter dominates their discourse. Of course, laughter may be every bit as common among her dangerous friends at church, but we want the kind of laughter that is barking and helpless and that arises from jaded bits of witty repartee. *Bon mots* about their acquaintances (not present, of course), about their parents, about their children, and, of course, about their spouses—all of this is the perfect, attractive package for what amounts to mean-spirited gossip, self-justification, and hatred.

This laughter is the portmanteau into which you will sneak new ideas. In this environment, with the pressures of children and housework lifted for an evening, she will laugh at things she doesn't think are funny, out of the need to assuage her loneliness, and out of a desire to make her evening out "really count." She will drink more than is wise and say things she doesn't mean. If she laughs with these people long enough, she will come to imply agreement with them even when she doesn't agree. Implied agreement will soon shift to true agreement. And all of this change can be accomplished smoothly, as smooth as wine gliding through lips and teeth.

Moved in laughter, a man may come to believe that abandoning his wife and humping anything he meets is not just understandable but a sign of joviality and manhood; a woman may come to believe that cheating her boss or hating her children is not only natural but impish and cute. Laughter is a Trojan horse into the human heart. In it, you may hide any soldier you choose, so long as you find the flavor of humor that suits a particular patient.

Already, your patient is saying things for a laugh that she would never say in sober judgment. It helps that her new old friends find her very clever. Because she is the wittiest in a group of apparently rather dull ladies (if wit can be judged by uncontrollable explosions of merriment), she can maintain the useful illusion that she's there in some way to influence *them*.

This bizarre confidence that she's somehow exerting influence will be very handy. She'll keep showing up to the parties because (she tells herself) "I'm the only Christian they know." And whenever she spends time with her church friends, she'll keep her discomfort at bay by telling herself that they are awfully sheltered from the "real world," by which she means her foolish and empty-headed school friends.

Passing herself back and forth, she can keep up a useful illusion. On the one hand, she is the dose of gritty reality for the prim, easy, boring (obedient) lives of her church friends. On the other hand, she is exposing her foolish godless friends to "the gospel." Never mind that she has only mentioned the Enemy once at these girls' nights, and that was in passing; she posts articles on Facebook that she thinks they might notice, and because of how "funny" she is with them, she thinks it likely that they think she's the coolest serious Christian they know, that she's paradigm shifting, that they didn't know Christians could be so likable!

In reality, her "friends" don't care what she calls herself, because she's never killed the vibe at a single wine night. In fact, they don't much care whether she keeps showing up. They will do what they do forever, until one of them quarrels with another and they go looking for new members (and they will easily find another group of moms who are up for evenings of complaint, gossip, and mild debauchery).

You want this wine night group to be increasingly the one she turns to for companionship. Do whatever it takes to remove her from the company of the dangerous women in her church. You've seen at a glance the alarming bulk of armor worn by these sorts of women, encircled as they are by the words and communions of the Enemy, by the attention and affection spent on their families, by their various occupations of mind and hand. We cannot get at their chastity; we cannot get at their opinions, either superficial or more deeply held; we cannot get at their sobriety, their fear-impulses. You really don't want your girl spending more time with such companions, because, obviously, these things can be catching.

But more on this next week.

Sincerely,
Madame Hoaxrot

20

On the Dangerous Household

My dear Hemlock,

As I mentioned in my last letter, there are several of the most dangerous kinds of households in your patient's church—worse luck for you. Some of our patients live a lifetime without stepping into even one of these places. And she has regular contact with three or four of them.

These households are presided over by a man with a woman at his side. There is a mysterious and noxious aroma between the man and wife that surrounds and envelops the children and anyone else who passes through the house. Their mundane physical comforts seem mixed up in it; that is why the woman herself sometimes seems to be the locus. The stench is horrible, emanating from the soup pot, the freshly made bed, the fire crackling in the hearth.

Your own patient was enlisted in a place like this. And these spots usually do seem to act as a sort of grassroots recruitment office. They are not more dangerous than a local church, exactly, but the absence of these places seems to affect the vitality of the local church operation. At any rate, we've found them to be devastatingly effective in galvanizing Enemy workers.

It is obvious that these homes are run by humans with a kind of hypnotic hold over each other. Something in it of the unfortunate kind of authority I already described to you when I wrote on parenting. But what else is in this bonding substance, and why has it been so difficult to re-create? It's not purely Rule of Power, obviously. We've all experienced Rule of Power in our own camps, and it never makes that smell.

This is something research is working on even now. On the face of it, the unifying doctrine these households belabor is the same one that thrust us inevitably onto the path of revolt. They give lip service to it, but we don't know what their interior motives are. If we could only intercept the message in the soup pot, we'd be well on our way, I believe.

We only know that such places are rightly called "strongholds."

Your job depends very much on limiting your patient's time in these households. She'll be attracted to them, despite what *you* may experience. But as I mentioned in my last letter, there is one very safe way of keeping her out: show the Patient her own inferiority. She won't always *like* the culture shock. She won't find it pleasant to sense that, right now, she's not strong enough and well enough to be a contributing part of what happens in these places. The role of beneficiary doesn't sit well with anybody. Drive in the wedge of felt inferiority so that she completely avoids contact, if possible.

Also, confuse her by making her suspect that the aroma in these homes arises out of peripheral comforts, *comforts she could never imitate*. You can bet that some of the nice things in these homes will be out of her reach because of money, talent, or another resource. You can take these details—an ingredient or piece of equipment she can't afford, a couch she will never own, a living room much larger than hers—and build a barrier out of them to prevent her taking any dangerous principles home to her little apartment.

She is female. This means that her mind is designed to think in terms of the whole picture, the "atmosphere," the setting. It's a side effect of her love of enriching the spaces around her, of "making things nice," as her husband would call it. The side effect is a very useful one to us—we can help her to conflate that love of beautification with a love for nicer and more expensive things, *things she does not have*.

She responds viscerally to any image of a physical environment that has been elevated. A photo of a beautiful woman, casually but impeccably dressed and sitting in a pristine bedroom, doesn't incite simple lust in her, as it might in a man.

It rather invites her to generate an entire story of a grand life, joyfully lived. She sees that image and thinks not just of pillows and sweaters and hardwood floors but of love and productivity and freedom. An image of a kitchen, large and perfectly appointed, evokes for her an entire world: friends, family, food, spiritual health, joy inexpressible.

It's relatively simple to help her to conclude that a big kitchen is *necessary* to reach those other things.

She lacks the imagination to see that most of the big beautiful houses she drives past are empty, both of people and of the Enemy aroma she is so entranced by. If she saw how little correlation there is between the aroma and the size of the house, the illusion would be gone. Maintain the illusion as long as you can by drawing her attention to the several families who happen to be generating the aroma *in* a nice big house. Then, her lack of a nice big house will become a stumbling block, right when she was about to LEARN something from these families. Just offer her an escape from conviction in the form of *of course*:

"Well, of course they love to have people over; they ought to, in a house like that."

"Well, of course she cooks for her family all the time; I would, too, in that kitchen."

"Well, of course she speaks kindly to her children; I bet they never leave things around the living room with those huge bedrooms upstairs."

"Well, of course they have Bible study every day. What an inspiring space to do family time in."

So you see, any part of a dangerous household that she might take home and learn from may be rendered innocuous by a gap in possessions. All kinds of environmental factors can be used in this way: a more charming husband, a more stable family of origin, or a more sanguine personality. Help your patient feel that the Enemy is not the *true* reason for another woman's happiness and that any obedience she sees in her can't be learned.

Avert her gaze from the possibilities and advantages that are piled up in her own life. Send her crawling back to the comforts of her wine night group. No conviction, no call to action, just blissful, easy come-as-you-are (and stay that way)!

Under no circumstances do you want her spending time with M.T., however—that woman who sits on the other side of the church. She is respectful to a husband who embarrasses her on a daily basis. She gives loving and grateful attention to her two-bedroom rental house and genuinely can't believe her good fortune to have a place of her own to beautify. She was given no natural advantages in her upbringing; she came to the faith as a teenager. She has a certain amount of daily pain from early onset arthritis. Yet her two children love and trust her. She has been good to them and has taught them simple faith out of the overflow from her own heart. She is cheerful and glad to be alive.

This woman offers no excuses to your patient, nothing but invitation. Keep them apart if you can possibly do it. Even the other dangerous households in the church—full of respectable husbands and fathers, material blessings, happy and receptive children—even these may not do quite so much damage to her as seeing a woman who is building a legacy without environmental helps.

Sincerely,
Madame Hoaxrot

21

On Church-Hopping

My dear Hemlock,

It's obvious she has totally rejected the wine night group in favor of the other more challenging sort of company. No need to try to shade this fact; we shall face the problem together.

The years pass so quickly, don't they? In answer to your question, I spent most of the last few seasons on a sort of vacation; Commander Helvetius led a little party to Southern India on a misery tour. No one wanted to leave, you may be certain! Of course the usual dramas erupted, but that simpering little Manneat will never get above herself again. We all had a marvelous time and were very glad when it was over.

To be sure, it's not sounding good for your patient and her children. How many does she have now, four? So she's countered the (usually rather easy to accomplish) maneuver about authority in the home? She's showing distressing tendencies to rather enjoy the company of her children?

From where I sit, it's clear her church was the culprit. You did (what was apparently) your best, and other influences simply won out. Don't stand there wiping your nose; take the offensive. Something, anything. Madame won't always be here to coddle you.

You might think church-hopping in a patient is a simple matter of theological shifts. It would be a reasonable mistake, I suppose, since a church is a theological institution. It makes sense on the face of it that, if you want to get a family to leave a church, all you need to do is achieve some movement in their theology.

It's not a bad instinct. But this is actually the least effective (and most difficult) method of creating a robust church-hopper.

Change a family's theological position, and you may achieve a change of church body. But it will most likely be the worst kind of departure, the one done honorably, with open communication—a public "in good standing" send-off with continued fellowship across ecumenical lines. They could easily continue to honor their old group and burn no bridges at all. And by giving them such a serious and weighty leave-taking, you may *strengthen* their sense of the commitment involved in church membership rather than weakening it. You may make it harder, not easier, for them to leave the next church.

I always say that, to get a family to leave a church in the right way, go after the woman. A church is, yes, a theological organization, but it is also a social organization. It contains many different power struggles, many complicated strings connecting many complicated people, individually, in couples, in groups, in groups within groups. And a woman with hurt feelings is one of the best ways to bust up a social group.

A slight between two women over who is going to plan the menu for the ministry thing—even this is enough! A rivalry, a dissension, a fit of anger, a political disagreement communicated in a passive-aggressive way—these little seeds are the easiest of all ways to divide people from each other. Or try a private sin (drunkenness, temper, marital strife, sexual sin, etc.) that is dealt with poorly (not confronted, confronted in condemnation, gossiped about, etc.).

Or how about this? You failed to make your patient shirk her duty of establishing parental authority. But even so, in parenting you will likely find a tender spot for personal offense.

She wants to do right by her children and love them well. But she still often measures her success against the approval or disapproval of others in her circle. This means that if she's around church people and her children behave properly, and the others see her children behaving properly, she really believes she is doing all right. If she grows used to getting praise and positive affirmation about her children (as compared to other children), she feels confident and confirmed in her faithfulness as a mother. But if she experiences the public embarrassment of her children misbehaving in front of others (as compared to other children), the embarrassment will drive her to despair or self-justification. If this goes on for a long enough season, she'll often begin to resent the entire group of people, the people who won't admire her children as they are.

Teach her to forget the eyes of the Enemy entirely in her cringing and preening awareness of the eyes of man. Rather than assessing her obedience against His book, against the promptings of His accursed Spirit, encourage her to assess it entirely using these mathematical symbols: <, >, =. *Are my children performing better, worse, or as well as these other children?* This rubric can replace the question of whether she herself is following Enemy instruction.

Her parenting will thus become one long plea for affirmation from others, a plea to be excused for failure and to be admired for success. Every private moment with her children will be overshadowed by the latest public performance. She will miss the pure enjoyment she may feel in them, in their personalities and voices and bodies. Every prayer to the Enemy for help will be cut off before it is of any use. She will not bear with obedience for long if it gets no "results"; she will not plead with the Enemy to give her love and stamina. She will simply react, again and again, to the vacillating experience of public approval and disapproval. Her children will get harsh lectures or mild rebukes, depending whether an offense carried immediate social consequence to their mother. The frustrations of such a woman are delicious, her insecurities tasty to the last drop. Her energies are futile and poured out for the enjoyment of us all.

A fretful woman in defense of her children will never stop. She will detect any slight and magnify it. She will watch every interaction and analyze it. She will defend any act, so long as her child is the actor. And she will leave as many churches as it takes to find the group who will appreciate her progeny.

But whether it's this particular line or some other sore spot you find and aggravate, the woman is always your best bet. The most entertaining thing in the world is watching a man make up a theological reason for leaving a church that his wife has long ago determined to leave because of hurt feelings. When a family leaves a church, eight times out of ten, they leave for reasons other than the ones stated. Throw a bone into the middle of their women, and you will sap strength from their men.

Sincerely,
Madame Hoaxrot

22

On Envying the Pastor's Wife

My dear Hemlock,

You seem to have stumbled into something worthwhile purely by accident (xoxoxo, I jest, of course).

No really, darling, your report on the situation with the new pastor's wife made for delightful reading. Pure comedy. This is the perfect answer to the question of how to pry this family out of their church.

So the Patient finds herself not liking the lady, is that so? She makes her uncomfortable, does she? Let's relish this gorgeous bout of feeling your patient experiences in the presence of the pastor's wife.

The new pastor breezes in and joins the staff at the smallish church your patient's family has been loyally attending for five or so years. The wine group long forgotten, the Patient has really found her place in this church. She and her husband have friends here. She's been learning to host people, and she enjoys sending nice little notes of encouragement to other ladies. She helps with various ministries. She feels that sometimes people *listen* to her.

Then, suddenly, the new pastor shows up, highly anticipated by all. The Patient meets his young, attractive wife with her four sweet children.

The new pastor's wife is, very naturally, the object of every dinner invitation. She is surrounded by eager-to-please potential friends. The Patient is at first among these enthusiastic women. Finally—she hopes—a kindred spirit! Someone who is a bit more cultured; someone who reads books! But she's disappointed to find that the pastor's wife doesn't instantly recognize her as a long-lost soulmate and friend. The pastor's wife, in fact, seems not to notice her fine qualities.

And then it begins to become clear that—even worse—all the other women at church have forgotten her fine qualities as well. They are too busy hanging on the lips of the new woman to notice our patient at all. The pastor's wife asks a favor—"I wonder if anyone would be willing to bring dessert to the Christmas party"—and immediately nine people jostle to respond first. The pastor's wife makes a comment, tells a story, details her own practices of child-rearing—and everyone standing in the circle is falling over themselves with admiration and respect!

If she were another type of woman, your patient would do the logical thing—fall in and feed at the rich springs of charisma pouring out of this new woman's bosom. Wait and work, leave gifts of tribute, ask advice and listen intently—in other words, actively pursue the inner circle represented by intimacy with the It Girl.

But your patient is not that kind of woman.

Your patient will never bring herself to become the fawning admirer of the pastor's wife. She cannot bear to see herself that way; she wants to see herself as a kind of peer, an equal. The traits she does share with this woman—interest in books, strong sense of humor, love of feeding people—rather than being the basis of friendship, are the basis of her strongest dislike.

This is the kind of soil in which we can almost always coax up a strong envious plant. Envy thrives among peers. The best seedbeds will be found between two sisters, two coworkers, two students near the top of the class, two artists, two wives whose husbands have the same job. Your patient has measured herself against the pastor's wife in all the areas of life she particularly values. And she has found herself lacking.

She feels the pain, but the pain is still confusing to her. She doesn't like the woman's company and doesn't like to hear the other women talk about her. She doesn't know why she dislikes her—and there's no need for her ever to know it. In fact, she is highly motivated *not* to know it.

But you know it. She dislikes the woman, not for her flaws, but for her perfections. She dislikes her, not for her differences, but for her similarities that are also superiorities. She dislikes her for being the best.

In order to admit the cause of her hatred, she would have to acknowledge the woman's superiority. She would have to say to herself, "This woman is kinder than I am. She is wiser than I am. Her children behave more nicely than mine do. She is even better-looking than I am. And I wish she were none of these things." Even one of these facts is as painful to her as a hot poker in the arm.

Now for the cream.

This case of envy, ripe and juicy and painful to bursting, is taking place in the context of a Christian church. This means that nobody in your patient's circle openly airs their envy. They aren't like the catty women of the world, who tear each other to shreds behind backs, who openly boast of being envied by their frenemies.

For your patient, careful concealment is the only possible option, and she may not even allow herself the relief of gossiping about the object of her envy. She is mystified by her own nasty feelings and can't bear to acknowledge them even to herself. So she will resort to churchifying her dislike. You must help her do this.

"I do hope the ministry stuff doesn't turn out to be too much," she might say with a concerned smile to a third party. "I know it's hard to be a pastor's kid; I know it gets busy for them." This sort of thing could be delivered in the form of a prayer, even, part of a plea for strength for the church leadership. Here she might insert the idea that the pastor's wife overextends herself a bit.

She could pass along a slightly less-than-flattering story, reasoning to herself that it was the pastor's wife herself she heard it from. But, of course, it sounded cuter when the pastor's wife told it. In her own mouth it might take on a shade more of a concerning quality.

She might offer compliments with a barb—"Your kids always wear such cute things; I know you love to shop!" The barb must be very subtle; it must only be a barb in a certain light and in a certain group of ladies.

That is how deep into the shadows the envy must go, in this church context.

This can only be advantageous, if you ask me. While you do sacrifice some of the more entertaining mudslinging, you gain such a satisfying subtlety, the kind of art in which women truly shine.

What's more, you gain an opportunity to hide the Patient's true malady even from herself. She could be brought to hate this woman, totally hate her, to find herself imagining scenarios of death or marital implosion, to picture true disaster in the woman's life, and to be ignorant of the cause of these bouts of destructive wishes. This could go on for years. It could poison every relationship the Patient has in her church—the place we are perhaps most eager to poison her relationships! It could also poison relationships between the pastor's wife and others and produce rivalries and dissensions galore. Your patient's one case of envy, nourished and coddled in secret, could be the pebble in the pond that every woman in their church feels the rocking effects of.

Do a spot of research, old gal, and let me know if there are others in the church who feel the same. Doubtless there are—the glory of a woman comfortable in her own skin is usually offensive to about half of the people who have to see it.

If we have allies, then we have opportunities for further "prayer requests" and the like.

Sincerely,
Madame Hoaxrot

23

On Bodily Affliction

My dear Hemlock,

It seems to me that this sort of question betrays a kind of impatience. You've only worked with her for twenty years or so; isn't that right? Is it getting to be too much for you? Just let me know—a demotion can certainly be arranged.

I suppose the latest failure has you feeling a bit restless. So the envy petered out after all? The pastor's wife gained a new loyal follower? All she needed to do was lean toward the Patient and ask for help with the nursing home ministry, and that was it, I see. One of my favorite comic plots, over before it really had time to begin. Your patient just wanted to be a petted little puppy, after all . . .

Yes, in answer to your question, it is perfectly possible to meddle with them physically. We've done it for years. You may not see your contemporaries doing this so often in the Western hemisphere. We find that it suits us better to lay a bit low and let them populate their world with atoms, theories, and medical histories instead of bogeys, spooks, and, well, demons.

But, yes, it's fairly common to mess about with the humans' bodies. The bore of it is that you have to make a petition across Enemy lines. Our Father Below tells us that this is a temporary measure. To let the Enemy think He has the upper hand, we still go through the motions (even our Father goes and sees the Enemy now and then and asks "permission" to do these sorts of things). But it's all for show, you see. The reports from headquarters explained all this eons ago.

Anyway, you go before Him, you swallow the pain and ask Him, and, if He says yes, you have lots of new options. You can make her sick, take some important possession away, cause a lost job or home or something. But let me just warn you: this kind of work often backfires. Sometimes the humans simply stiffen their necks against you and go crawling off to Him. Sometimes they seem shockingly impervious and grow even stronger under these kinds of attacks.

You also may find yourself getting carried away and asking to be allowed to kill your own patient! This is an obvious sign of frenzy in a caseworker. I have seen agents kill one of their patients when it was patently obvious that they were an Enemy worker and would therefore be a total loss. It's easy to get carried away. Don't think this can't happen to you; the power can go to your head very quickly when you start getting involved physically. Suffering is all fun and games until you end up in a skirmish you can't win. (And then, of course, sometimes the Enemy denies your request only to kill them Himself shortly thereafter and take them directly into His wretched bosom.)

Fine, give her fibromyalgia as an experiment, or some other vague and tiresome complaint, if you must. But don't come crying to me when He just twists it to His advantage—or if you have to go through the whole rigmarole of applying and He just says no.

Sincerely,
Madame Hoaxrot

24

On the Sinister Growth of Gratitude

My dear Hemlock,

So you went for it, did you? You petitioned and were somehow granted access; I suppose I should congratulate you. You got the husband fired—and I must admit, if you were going to try this kind of thing, your instincts were rather good. The slow burn of inconvenience is usually better for our ends than crushing disaster.

But take care at this juncture. It's clear from your descriptions that another spreading disease has taken over your patient's soul like gangrene. You write moldering, bewildered complaints about the distressing state of her marriage, about her growing habit of spending entire days in joyful occupation with her children and housework, about her increasing neglect of covetousness, fretting, and irritation. The problem is obvious to me, and don't imagine you can redirect my attention. You've allowed an outrageously weedy crop of gratitude to spring up.

She's come to believe herself essentially *fortunate*. Somehow, it has seeped into her mind that her life is exceptionally good, that it used to be quite bad, and that the Enemy alone is responsible for the change. She has developed a kind of permanent memory of what her life might have been without His intervention. She wakes up in the morning like a convict who was sprung from prison at the final hour; she wakes up like a Cinderella who was snatched from a sooty hearth and placed in the loving embrace of a king's family. Somehow, the arrows of gratitude passed through any defenses erected by her own demanding flesh (I have no illusions about any defensive work done by yourself), and she sees the enormity of the Enemy's embarrassing, lavish favoritism.

He *is* a parent with favorites, never forget it. She's become aware of her status with Him—a status He never deigned to share with the likes of our race. Did He take on OUR form? No; but it was always His way. He is the sort of father who makes one coat of colors when there are twelve sons, who kills a fatted calf for the degenerate and not for the obviously deserving. He is a father to some, a stern master to others. Has there ever been a rhyme or reason? The heart revolts; the lip curls at this sort of behavior.

And to see this filthy two-legger gloating to herself over His regard and blessing! I would put her eyes out myself if I could.

Anyway, the gratitude is spreading, and all of her life is beginning to flush with a kind of warm light. Her husband's flaws seem dim to her; she's been humbled to the point that she no longer believes her marriage was "down." She seems to have come to terms with her husband as a man, a human man, a companion and friend and coworker and lover, but a sort of brother too. She's obviously caught up in the illusion that this husband of hers is an acceptable and even welcome assignment for a woman such as herself. She's looking at the kids the same way. The house, too—that ramshackle little house has somehow been transformed into just another tool in her hand, an unforeseen piece of good fortune.

She does, however, seem to dimly understand that she's between crises. While the job loss is not yet producing quite the effect you'd hoped, she does seem to suspect that, eventually, something very difficult may come. How right she is! The Enemy's supposed kindness is always short-lived, even for the favored human creatures. But you would be making a mistake if you thought that your hope lies in real calamity coming to her and shaking this sense of well-being. The real work doesn't have to do with big-C Calamity; *it has to do with pulling her back to the old way of life so that she reevaluates small calamities.*

Don't neglect to cash in on the job loss; this sort of maneuver relies heavily on follow-through.

Right now, the true problem is that she skates through minor irritating events. The idea that her "Father" is really *good* to her seems to be less and less shakable, seems to constantly outweigh any inconvenience in her life. At the moment, she takes every circumstance as part of the whole—further evidence that she is *loved.* Even the sleepless nights with her newest child are an adventurous proof that she's being allowed to *do* things; they are an opportunity to look at her baby in the half-light streaming in from the bathroom.

So you need to leverage that job loss to bring her back to the old accounting system. In the old system, every small annoyance—coming from her husband, her church, her children, even from an appliance on the countertop—is fresh evidence that she is an innocent sufferer of indignity and hardship. A new challenge is met with "Perfect. *This too!*" and filed away under the heading of Things I Don't Deserve. Offenses compound. The dishwasher leaks, the baby wakes early from his nap, the child disobeys, the husband neglects to take out the trash—and she pretends to be surprised but was actually anticipating it, just waiting for fresh proof of her mistreatment. *Isn't this just typical?* she thinks.

And the mistreatment—never mistake her—*is really being charged to the Enemy, above all.* When she grumbles under her breath for days at a time, she thinks she is grumbling at the people in her house or outside of it, or swearing at the inanimate objects that make life hard. But He is really the one she is shaking a fist at.

Why has HE *brought this into my life? Why has* HE *given me a husband with a poor salary, one who loses jobs, one who doesn't know how to fix things in the house? Why has* HE *given me friends who don't value my time, children who bicker and complain? Why has* HE *always thwarted my desires and punished me for doing what I must to ease the burdens of life?*

This is the real meaning of mutterings like the ones she used to have always on the tip of her tongue; it is the real gesture behind the old impatient jerking about of a wooden spoon or a car seat.

And this is what you lost, when you neglected to take note of her growing belief that, actually, He has showered "good things" on her head, beginning with her forcible rescue from the supposed jaws of death. While this idea took root and began to spread, you sat on your hands and waited for "something hard" to come and open her eyes to His real nature.

But you look at everything, as usual, the way a foolish woman does. They believe that gratitude is a natural response to "good things" and that bitterness is a natural response to "bad things." You hope for more bad things, bigger bad things, to guide her on the path to bitterness as in the past. But the level of hardship is not the point and was never the point.

The bitter woman has made the habit of thinking she is ill-used, and it doesn't matter how ill the usage. The flat tire or the unfaithful husband alike are simply new evidence to her that she is fundamentally unfortunate and has a right to be angry.

The grateful woman is grateful around and between and throughout every hard season. In the end, a hard season only serves to strengthen her faith and gratitude. She is in the habit of responding a certain way, and *the habit doesn't simply disappear because her blasted husband lost his blasted job.*

So let me tell you, as you try to draw my attention to your "victory" in the job thing—you missed the point and made a real error when you allowed her to start laughing over spilled milk. She may have a little wobble over the lost job. Certainly she will pray earnestly about it, lay awake one or two nights. But unless you really understand your game now, this trial is no more likely to shake her in the long term than a burnt dinner.

Her pernicious habit will be unseated by your own intervention, not by her change in circumstances, especially if she really is what she appears to be now—relentlessly, militantly, obstinately cheerful. If she has discovered the secret of bringing her sense of good fortune into all hardship, great and small, you will find yourself in a very tight spot indeed. And if these instincts harden into a conscious recognition that life will continue to ask her to make a decision between two responses—gratitude or bitterness—you will have lost an access point that, in some ways, represents the whole battle. Indeed, I could go so far as to say that you will have lost the soul.

Sincerely,
Madame Hoaxrot

P.S. One thing you may look in on is the fear of sickness or other disaster. In the middle of good times, some women are more vulnerable to a belief that things are a little “too good” and can be encouraged to expect the “other shoe” to drop. Your patient, for instance, seems to have had a longstanding fear of cancer since the children came along. Let her dwell on that. It’s a way to continually sneak in the pessimist’s conviction that the Enemy probably intends harm after all.

25

On Empathy

My dear Hemlock,

Of course there's still work to be done. Don't be daft. If the game was up with her, you and I would not still be corresponding in this friendly way.

In fact, her new habit of encouraging other women opens some new avenues to you. I want to recommend a method we call Boundless Empathy. You'll be employing a feature of the feminine mind and body that is, on the face of it, eminently dangerous to us. They call it "empathy" now, but it's as old as Eve herself. "Empathy" is their new word for the act of sharing in the emotions of another human creature.

The female is built in such a way that she does this almost without meaning to. She sees a person crying, and tears spring to her eyes. She hears her baby whimpering, and her whole wretched body responds. When her friend describes a painful experience, she herself actually experiences some level of pain.

You can imagine why the Enemy might have designed her this way. If He wanted to make her a subservient day laborer, forced into slavery and service for her husband and her children, what better way to fit her for the job? Human babies are helpless; she knows what her baby needs without a word. Her elderly neighbor falls and breaks a hip; she imagines the pain of isolation and brings meals and children to visit. Her instincts here can have a dangerous mobilizing effect. The empathy can drive her to action.

But if we get a handle on the modern values attached to this female instinct, we find that it can be used for better ends. What you want is for the empath's impulse to exceed the bounds of justice and truth. That is all.

Thus, imagine the scene: Her friend declares that she is being mistreated by a third party. Her husband is rude. Her mother-in-law has done such and such. Her boss is insane. Your patient is called upon to respond, and with the empath's instincts, she rushes to inhabit the emotions of the suffering party.

"I'm so sorry!" she says. "That must be hard. I can't believe they said that to you."

And you see, without even a pause, your patient can be led to skip the part about *assessing whether the sufferer's claims are true.* In a moment, you have embroiled her in a ready-made emotional tangle that you didn't even have to generate in her own life. Simply by entering into the emotion of another person, in an act that looks very much like mercy, she will arrive at an advanced state of anger, outrage, sadness, or frustration. And she will do this without stopping to ask a single question about whether the perceptions of the suffering individual are accurate.

In other words, by utilizing Boundless Empathy, you can teach her to ignore the facts of a given case. Then you can lead her to give advice—spiritual, relational, and practical advice—that may be deeply unhelpful and even morally wrong. Give her a nudge during her one-on-one "ministry" conversations, just a little nudge, and her natural feminine ability will do the rest of the work. Remember, she comes fresh out of the box with a strong capacity to feel with another person. What you want is to take this natural instinct and encourage her to start seeing empathy as *the highest possible duty, the highest possible good.* She can even be brought to see empathy as essentially *the same thing* as helping.

In the long run, empathy can become a substitute for either physical assistance (meals or mercifully timed babysitting) or spiritual assistance (praying with someone, offering a word of advice from the Book that might invite her friend out of the quagmire of emotion, etc.). Her "help" can be reduced to a one-size-fits-all program of listen and agree, listen and agree. And, in the end, you get two people swimming about in emotional backwater instead of one.

Here's the thing *you* must remember about human emotion that you want *them* to forget entirely: the Enemy apparently intended emotions to be handmaidens to the creatures, not masters. I believe emotions are supposed to be used as a kind of thermometer, an indicator light. Emotional pain arrests their attention and forces them to deal with a problem. But the emotions themselves are sometimes untrustworthy—a woman may "feel" that her mother-in-law is sinning against her grossly, when in fact her feeling has been caused almost entirely by a bad night's sleep. To get to the bottom of an emotion is often only the first step in finding out what is "true" in a given situation.

Now, the Enemy, in His tyranny, is forever on the obsessive mission of imposing Cosmos and stamping out Chaos. Thus, He would have them surrender their viewpoint to His idea of what is "true" and what is "real." He's made them in such a way that they are constantly oppressed and disadvantaged unless they cut with the grain of what HE says is "right," "good," and "lovely." They cannot choose their own path, really, without finding themselves victims to His law of gravity (if they walk off of a cliff), His law of love (if they abandon commitments or even lightly oppress those they are responsible to care for), His laws of anatomy, physiology, and psychology (if they experiment with unnatural uses of food, drink, sex, exercise, etc.).

The humans are quite aware of the potential of disease or disorder when it comes to the body. But for some reason, it's easy to get them to forget the possibility of disorder when it comes to the mind and the emotions. Repress the obvious thought that some emotions—and the fervent beliefs that accompany them—simply do not reflect what is "true" in the oppressive sense meant by the Enemy.

And that's the most important thing we've accomplished with the Boundless Empathy program: we've provided new grounds for the humans to disregard the question of whether a given emotion is in step with the Enemy's "reality." This program, usually utilized with the female, is just a fresh on-ramp to the idea that the *individual has the right to define reality*. We typically find it is quite easy to help women make the jump from "emotions are real" to "emotions are the *most* real."

Another advantage, outside of stymieing her "ministry" efforts, is that you can invite her to bring this idea home from the coffee date. In the course of teaching her to front-load the emotional state of others, you may also get her to do the same with her own emotions. Then *she* will become the one demanding that others make allowances for and bow down to her passions. You can imagine the openings to your helpful advice that will result when reality depends on how she feels in a given moment! Nice work if you can get it (and you can get it if you try).

Yes, her "ministry" work may indeed be the unorthodox path to such a victory. Even in the throes of her pernicious habit of gratitude, your woman could be made to feel somewhat embarrassed by her own blessing. She could eventually learn to abandon it entirely, if you will bring her by degrees to see the gratitude as an insult to the suffering friend.

Even you should be able to make use of this program.

Sincerely,
Madame Hoaxrot

P.S. There is another side of this coin, if you find that empathy doesn't happen to be her thing . . .

26

On Job's Comforting

My dear Hemlock,

It isn't so very complicated, my pet. Clearly, she's not the empath we (you) took her for; she obviously leans the other way. Perhaps she had prior warning on the method. Or perhaps all that ministry work in the last few years inoculated her—too many people with too many sob stories. Whatever the case, it seems that Boundless Empathy is a nonstarter. Anyone can follow a fad; it takes experience to execute a custom-tailored temptation.

You made a throwaway comment that she seems to be progressing nicely in self-righteousness, which suggests the alternate tack I'd like to try: Job's Comforting.

Like most people who err on a particular side of an issue, she is happily on her guard against the very ditch she's least likely to fall into. She has defended herself well against Boundless Empathy, but the opposite ditch is quite unguarded.

Here is what it looks like. She goes to see a woman who is suffering. She sits and listens to her, and she wears her sympathy face, developed just for such an occasion. The other woman describes the difficult situation, often with tears (which your patient doesn't ever seem to share). She listens. But as she listens, her mind is working. Soon, she arrives at her theory about what is "really happening."

"I have cancer." *She must have lived for years on an unhealthy diet.* Or—*She trusted her diet to save her, and now God is helping her to see her error.*

"My spouse is abusive, and I'm seeking a divorce." *Well, since when is there really an innocent party in divorce? No person is totally innocent of sin against their spouse, and the term "abuse" is vastly overused these days, so this woman is probably also exaggerating the dangers of the situation.*

"My child is wayward." *She raised him wrong. Train a child up in the way he should go, and he won't depart from it. Ergo, if he departs from it, the training must not have taken place.* (Her own children are clearly healthy and doing well, and it is inconceivable to her that they will make bad choices.)

"I lost my job." *She says she lost her job because of layoffs or because of religious persecution, but if she had made herself truly essential at work, this wouldn't have happened.*

"I have chronic pain." She *thinks about her health too much; she's a hypochondriac. If she would take control of her mind or body, the pain would probably go away.*

The thing is, she's been helping people for a long time now, and the generalizations almost always prove to be true. Usually, there is more to the story than what a suffering person tells. Again and again, once she's learned more about a situation, she has found more culpability than was at first presented. This has made her wary and a little jaded about suffering—and grateful also to have a shortcut for sorting through people's stories. She can render judgment quickly and efficiently by using previous stories as case studies, without too much troublesome "listening."

Boundless Empathy? Not for her! If you do your job well, she'll avoid the ditch of assuming the sufferer is *always right* by diving headlong into the ditch of assuming the sufferer is *always wrong.*

She believes she's being insightful, that when she pauses a moment and asks that perfect, leading question to the sufferer, she's doing her duty. But she doesn't know how little life she brings to the truly innocent sufferer. It's clear to them that their pain can never reach her, because she's made herself unavailable to it.

The key here is to remind her often of all the other conversations she's been through, and make sure to remind her that, after this one, there will be many more—she cannot possibly carry the weight of really feeling for all of them, listening to all of them. It's too much. Guard her thoughts from the logical idea that the Enemy never asked her to listen to all of them at once; He sends each moment of need individually and expends Spiritual help for each challenge as it comes.

And if that fails, you will always have a still stronger motive in your back pocket. Remind her that, if she were to admit to the possibility of innocent human suffering, she would have to accept a most terrifying proposition.

She would have to admit that it could happen to her.

To admit that the "loving" Creator of the Universe may intentionally bring about suffering that wrecks the life you had and gives you a different sort of life—*and that there isn't anything you can do to prevent it*—is more than the human can rationally handle.

To admit that her friend's husband cheated and left, and that her friend did nothing to cause this, is to admit that her own husband might cheat and leave. To admit that her friend lost her health, despite willpower and wise living, is to admit that she might lose her health. To see that children can be raised up in the "admonition of the Lord" and still stray is to admit that her own darling children might reject Him!

Whatever the deepest desires of her heart are, these are the things she will most carefully erect systems to protect. *I can't admit that your loss is simply loss*, she will say to the suffering friend, *because if I do that, I open the door to the wild thought that, sometimes, things happen and there is no "explanation" in this life. It means I must really hope in another life.*

And because of this, much of her ministry will be rendered ineffective, praise be to Our Father Below. She will never slip into doing something truly outrageous, like "weeping with those who weep." By refusing to examine the possibility of innocent suffering among her friends—and by refusing to engage the Enemy in impassioned prayer on their behalf—she will also be increasingly filled with dread for the future. She will be rendered less ready, not more ready, to walk through suffering when He brings it to her own door. She'll also be increasingly hard-hearted when she does encounter the "sin behind the suffering" that you will encourage her to continually sniff out in other people's lives.

And so, managed thus, she will grow more pleased with herself from year to year, even while she is growing more out of touch with the sufferings of others.

And then—what delight and what pleasure—when she finally gets hit like a brick with innocent suffering of her own! How fun it is, Hemlock, to watch them scramble for their dignity when it's not only suffering but false guilt they have to contend with. That horrible moment when they have to find a narrative that fits it all together! And the fun we have, picking over the remains of their faith in a God who never does what you thought He'd agreed to!

She may come to see the truth—that He is an Enemy who keeps asking for things nobody can give.

Sincerely,
Madame Hoaxrot

27

On Aging and the Unfortunate State of Her Marriage

My dear Hemlock,

I've written little in the past few years; perhaps you've noticed.

I waited, mostly because you seem so unconscionably pleased with yourself with so astonishingly little reason that I wanted to give you time to see the true fruits of your labor before sending you this hint. Your superiors don't see the situation in quite the same light. Always with the deepest affection, of course, my dear!

Let's review the facts of your patient's case. Her children trust her and listen to her input as they prepare to start leaving the nest. She respects and enjoys her husband—this, the same man she used to think it a "mistake" to have married! She is content to be an ordinary member of her church, and she thinks nothing of seeing her fellow Enemy-subordinates two or even three times a week, whether at services or in homes. She is wasting a good deal of time cooking and cleaning. She keeps reading the Enemy's book. She incessantly prays and sometimes even sings, alone with her housework. She has, in fact, become a respectable and rather dangerous Christian lady, nearing middle age and apparently not even much concerned about all the sagging skin and frizzy hair.

Did I miss anything?

And your last letter (thank you for taking time out of your obviously busy workday to bring me this wheedling report about how you have stolen a bit of her joy by introducing new worries about her college-bound daughter!) neglects to take in any of this pertinent information.

It seems clear that her marriage is the root of all this nasty holiness. The marriage is out of hand. I write to warn you sternly not to let this matter go; it must be addressed.

Somehow the thing snuck up on you from behind. I hesitate to say what kind of negligence leads a tempter to overlook one of the most basic relationships in a patient's life. You take the thing for granted, obviously, much like the creatures themselves.

Somehow, in the last ten years, the challenges of life have led them to learn communication, repentance, and mutual grace, rather than stubbornness, bitterness, and resentment. You never did manage to develop all the minor offenses into a seedbed for major transgression and betrayal.

The sex problem is clearly back. Did it ever really leave? They keep doing this thing, even as their bodies age and grow rather fat. It was hideous and uncomfortable for you before, when their bedroom antics were youthful and infatuated and inexperienced. Now, matured into a place of mutual service and disciplined delight, the bedroom is really a place I'd advise you to simply stay out of. I'm saying this not just because I've completely given up any faith in your competence to DO something about it (I have) but because I truly believe that, in this advanced state of things, it's not worth the trouble. You wouldn't be the first demon who elects to just stay away till it's over.

But now the delight creeps into other times and places as well. They persist in laughing together, over the children that used to often move them to mutual blame. They seem almost oblivious to the insult and inconvenience represented by a sock left on the floor, a trash bag left on the back stoop.

The distressing habit I warned you about—her praising him and thanking him for ordinary acts of service—has borne unfortunate spiral effects of mutual regard. Rather than bitterly waiting for the next inevitable demand, he seems almost to seek out ways of getting her to look at him with that bright smile. And at her age, too!

The trust that seems to have grown up is insufferable. They draw a great deal of quiet satisfaction from each other's familiar presence and dependable character. But at the same time, each of them seems to be asking one another for a smaller percentage of their overall satisfaction in life. They seem increasingly preoccupied with that *other* place. And now that they are both rather less rooted in the earth than ever, they are illogically more content to sit quietly in a room together, more likely to laugh, more likely to sing.

I am half inclined to let you fend for yourself from here on out. But, I suppose, if I must give you something, I'll say just this. If I were you, I'd be focusing my efforts on getting the Patient to think with fear of the midlife change coming upon her.

The children have lined up at the edge of the nest and are beginning to jump off, one by one. The joy and pain of this is excruciating to her. She is going through the kind of identity change that last happened during those few years when her husband put a ring on her finger and the first child entered and exited her womb. The children perplex her more than ever before. How to help them take flight? After all the years of oversight, how to shift into a new role of advisor? How to fill her time? How to serve only one other person in the house instead of a host of them?

Her aging seems not to bother her sufficiently. Her face is sagging, and her hair is graying and curling up. Yet she seems not to be properly cowed by the anguish of death. And the death of admiration for her beauty, which has come on slowly for fifteen or twenty years but which is fully in effect now—she kicked a bit at the beginning but now seems to have accepted it without a murmur.

Did you simply forget to help her murmur about this?

She was the perfect candidate for foolish, vain middle age. How did you manage to pass over the entertainment of creating a woman who seeks to turn back a clock that won't turn?

You will probably tell me that death itself tied your hands. I agree. It's insupportable, after He denied your recent requests to mess about with her body, that He did so Himself—giving her the chronic pain after all and then using it for His own dastardly ends. Through the constant physical and emotional difficulty of that pain, He has done His own work. It seems obvious that facing this pain has really caused her to face death.

The sight of her own mortality did all kinds of damage. It has clearly gone a long way toward curing her of the Job's Comforting you hoped to entrench in her. But it also seems to have cured her of vanity; she simply doesn't feel the appropriate shock, even when she looks in the mirror and sees skin literally falling off the bones.

Death is never a real friend. I always say that the less the humans think of death, the better. Death instructs them when it is faced head-on. Only when it is skirted around can it be really beneficial. A human pretending she won't die is a human who fears death.

See if you can't—although it is quite late in the game—get her to start avoiding thoughts of death as it nears. Perhaps you could also encourage her to neglect her duties as the kids leave the house? Sometimes this is a useful period for reigniting old distractions and insecurities. Discourage her from asking what the Enemy intends her to do with this new season. And when she is no longer a busy servant, she *may* be successfully invited back into the vanity she's been too busy to think of. Encourage her, when the identity of "active mother" goes away, to look around for another identity marker. It could be that she makes another grab at her lost beauty or starts going around getting interested in everybody's business (a busybody, you might say), or perhaps you could get her addicted to much wine.

In fact, you should make a push for a renewed vanity, because it would become one of the ways she tries to "skirt" impending death. Set her to work trying to prevent "it"—with creams and operations, by rubbing her face with a tiny marble rolling pin. Never let her ask what "it" is exactly that she is going to prevent. Wrinkles and age spots? Death? They can get mixed together in a pleasingly muddled way. You may even get her to try a diet or supplement that explicitly promises to delay death—all to distract her from the stark idea that, no matter what, her efforts will eventually fail with 100 percent certainty.

Alternately, thinking about aging could lead her to give up entirely, to put her limbs into retirement when they still work quite well. Perhaps frumpery, gluttony, and idleness could be her new self-identity as she realizes the futility of trying to bring back those youthful attractions.

Anything's worth trying once,
Madame Hoaxrot

28

On the Diagnosis

Poor dear Hemlock,

The diagnosis has filled you with panic, I can see. And well it should.

She drove herself home from the "routine" mammogram in a stupor of surprise and fear. She and the husband quite naturally clung to one another and cried. The kind of prayer produced in such moments is often the noxious kind you witnessed that night, blind as a babe in its groping, automatic need.

A human knows her need in such moments, faced with a real trial. Anyone who belongs to the Enemy seems to have at least one initial rush of clarity about their proximity to death, combined with fear that leads to infantile prayer and sometimes even a burst of joy at the realization that perhaps they will be *going* soon. The Enemy's attendance is usually felt with terrifying potency on such occasions. Do not let that bit surprise you either. The white-hot presence you sensed that night in their room, as they clasped hands and bent heads—it may return at other times, but don't let that alarm you unduly. And don't be alarmed by the odd refreshment they both seemed to feel as they straightened and looked each other in the eye. They still have a long walk ahead, a long walk through the valley of the shadow of death, and He often leaves them vulnerable to attack for several sections of this valley.

You have some opportunity left, although you're under the disadvantage of not knowing His plans any more than the quivering humans do. Will He snatch her away soon, or after a three-year fight, or in thirty more years, in a nursing home? Hard to say. But you can be sure that, no matter what, this crisis will absolutely outlast her cheerful assurance of the moment. In fact, far from being the moment to give up, *this is the moment for a frenzied burst of effort on your part.*

Already you see some roads opening up to you. They had to call the children home, and there, watching a movement of stifled terror on their faces, your patient experienced her first dark regrets. She tried to show them the fearless, prayerful lady of the night before, to lead them into a similar experience of hope and joy. "I am not afraid," she wanted to say to them. But somehow the words never would come in that angelic way. Rather, she cried again—she'd meant not to. She broke down as she looked at the one pregnant daughter's belly, at the curly hair of the other son just settled in his new job.

She felt suddenly that, far from being grown and independent, her children still need her. She saw that the Enemy wasn't perhaps going to give her the time she thought He'd promised. No, not promised exactly. But was the promise not implied when He gave these children into her care in the first place? Why give them to her and then so unnaturally tear them away from the reach of her help and advice?

Since that second night, the cold physical realities have begun to set in, and I have no doubt you are already making plans to indwell these realities. Certainly you want to begin early to exacerbate the terrors of physical suffering. You will soon see her spiritual bliss begin to flag as she gets her first glimpses into what this season could mean. The surgeries, the long appointments, the frigid treatment rooms. The simple losses, horrors to a woman, like a sick inverted review of pregnancy, when her body stretched and puffed in the processes of life. Her hair is trimmed short, then still shorter, and then taken under the razor. Her face grows puffy; her eyebrows are gone. Everything about flesh that you've always detested will begin to irk you less as you watch the corruption of her body overwhelm her.

Here you want the shock of these surreal things becoming real to draw her mind away from that early glimpse of Heaven and Himself. She will be surprised. Even if she always knew about death, always believed it would come, always recited the verses about death having no sting—she will still be surprised. Push this surprise down into the deep part of her heart at every turn. Encourage her to think that, rather than being a physical confirmation of the creeds she has asserted for all these years, somehow the physical pains and indignities of death give the lie to all these former assertions.

Yes, she said that death would be swallowed up in victory, but now she's in death's valley. Help her see how death was always going to be the final victor. Her pain is unmasking the real true nature of the universe. The universe is brutal, after all, full of suffering, loss, and ultimate defeat. She will be trying to see through the haze of pain, to believe that death will reveal the meaning of things she's heard her whole life. The Enemy keeps claiming to answer the challenge of death. He keeps telling them about how He sent the Enemy Son to defeat death, and she's affirmed the joy of this for years. But now death looks her in the eye, and she immediately wonders if *this* death could have been the one He meant.

Encourage her to preoccupy herself inordinately with her children's need and suffering. Do your best to drag her back into those early years when she wanted only to shield them from pain. Don't allow her to dwell on the possible intentions the Enemy might have for *them* in this time of uncertainty. Teach her to think of herself as indispensable.

And, of course, you will also have a chance for one final play of an old trick. Whenever a patient is in transition, we take advantage of it to shut down their productivity and gum up the works of their prayer. When they know a big change is coming (a move, a new job, a wedding, a baby, a church plant), they can be brought to waste many months refusing to engage with the current reality because they know another reality is on its way. So you have single women waiting in perfect idleness to be married, a job being done shoddily while men wait to find out if they got the new job, homes falling into chaos while a new home is under contract.

Here, your patient is unsure how long she will be staying in this life. Of course, you might find her driven to catch up with tasks and people, making amends right and left and setting affairs in order. But if you can lead her another way, you might enjoy seeing her unable to minister to anyone or work for anything until she "knows" what will happen. As if that time will ever come, even in her last moments!

One thing you need to give serious thought to, my dear, is how much time do *you* have?

Sincerely,
Madame Hoaxrot

29

On Your Failure

Hemlock,

So it's all over then. You know what is next for you.

The awful truth is that she has walked out of your clutches and into the halls of Heaven itself and will probably drag a dozen or so people with her in the end.

How many of them were witnesses to your defeat? They saw it all!

They saw her move her lips, to the very end, in habitual intimacies with the Enemy. They saw her initial fears, her constant surprises as she encountered new diagnoses and new pains, new losses of strength and ability, new indignities and dates and numbers—they saw her struggle, mourn, cry out, deny, and eventually cling to old promises. They saw her meet the stages of death with strange, quiet smiles. They saw her secret, in the end: she actually believed what she was saying all this long while.

None of those who stood in the room of grief will be unchanged; you, in your failures, have made work harder for dozens of your compatriots.

You even lost your audience with her, in the end; you were repelled and injured by that hateful white-hot cloud hovering by the deathbed. You saw with clawing pain how her friends and family, also sitting within the range of that cloud, breathed it freely and seemed only stronger for it. You heard them sing songs of power, even with the angel of death standing nearby. Your ears burst with pain, didn't they? Someone told me they saw you wandering around in the street outside for days at a time near the end. Driven out of the house, I suppose.

You saw confusion on the faces of human family members who are well in our hands; confusion over the dismay and despair they expected to find when they, against all impulse, visited to take final leave of their sister, aunt, or friend . . . and you saw your beleaguered coworkers creep close to their patients to try to explain the unexplainable. How can we help a human understand what we don't understand ourselves? How can death be gain? How can He make it easy for some of them when it is so hard for others? How can human suffering backfire and send off sparks of horrific aromas and lightnings and pernicious smoke, even as the humans themselves have no idea at all of what precisely will happen to them when they cross through the veil?

And she! In one moment, the beeping monitors, the sour smell of morphine, the surreal view of her papery white hands on the familiar coverlet that she sewed with the same hands thirty years ago, the tender whispers of an older daughter comforting a younger daughter in the room, the slow loss of consciousness—all of it gave way in an instant.

Like a shroud, like a hospital gown, like a weight, off dropped the life that was passing away, and suddenly her naked soul was being clothed anew. She heard the warm welcome and song from Enemy workers. (I heard you even suffered a glimpse of your old friend from before the revolution! Harsh are the wages of failure indeed.) She saw the faces of her mother, her childhood neighbor, her husband's grandfather.

She saw you; you shrank back like a coward before her glance. I told you woman was like that, under all the sad disarray. This is what they look like when He is done with them: the mantle, the color, the light, queenly grace and self-forgetful beauty; you never saw it before, I suppose. Yes, this is what they become in the end. And by then, I suppose, she had caught sight of Him. You can't pretend to comprehend what happened to her after that.

She is now forever beyond the reach of your advice, your condemnation, your feeding mouth, and the well-executed pains of a world groaning under the authority of our Father's

Chaos. You will never again have any part in her life. You will never again be offered a chance to earn the taste of the *morceau savoureux* that is woman.

I have my instructions. You understand the position you've placed all of us in; it's for your own good as well as the good of the greater.

Ah, Hemlock. My poor, sad, sad, pathetic little duckling. My sugar pie, honeybun, sweeting, pumpkin, cookie. My bonbon, cupcake, *petite bouchée.*

I am coming over tonight with a small party of close friends. We intend a house party, a dinner party. Thank you in advance for hosting. Commander Helvetius sends her regrets; she won't be joining, but I promised her a bit of the leftovers.

I can't pretend that I didn't suspect from very early on that this would be the conclusion of your modest assignment. But I could never bring myself to regret it. From our first meeting, I have felt such a stirring attraction to you. I enjoyed our association and will also enjoy the termination of it.

But I will say, between ourselves, that as a mentor I am heartily glad to be rid of you. You were dead weight, to be quite honest. No offense, darling! You weren't even really bad enough to be notable.

So I expect that my enjoyment of you, and the enjoyment of the party, will be just the sort of inattentive enjoyment that one would expect from an insipid course, eaten with a kind of half-hearted relish. The slow stripping of your scraps, the leisurely ripping apart of your essence—this will afford us the same kind of satisfaction one might get from consuming a half-baked potato. Even in your absorption, you will be the kind of forgettable meal that prompts one to say, the next morning, "What was it we had last night?"

Do—I only ask this for your sake, to spare you the embarrassment—do try to keep a lid on the boring convention of pleas for mercy, negotiations, irritating cries of torment, etc. etc. . . .

Take your punishment, I always say; take it like a woman.

Sincerely, XOXOXO,
Madame Hoaxrot

Acknowledgments

Thanks so much to the Canon team, particularly Brian and Ethan. Ethan, thank you for being just the scalpel this book needed.

Thanks to the early readers; you know who you are.

Thanks to Justin for being the ballast.

Thanks to Clive Staples; no one should attempt this sort of thing, but we just can't help it.

Thanks to God Incarnate, the Enemy of the enemy of our souls.